how2become

Numerical Reasoning Tests

www.How2Become.com

As part of this product you have also received FREE access to online tests that will help you to pass Numerical Reasoning assessments

To gain access, simply go to:

www.MyPsychometricTests.co.uk

Get more products for passing any test at:

www.How2Become.com

Orders: Please contact How2Become Ltd, Suite 14, 50 Churchill Square Business Centre, Kings Hill, Kent ME19 4YU.

You can order through Amazon.co.uk under ISBN: 9781912370474, via the website www.How2Become.com or through Gardners.com.

ISBN: 9781912370474

First published in 2018 by How2Become Ltd.

Typeset by Katie Noakes for How2Become Ltd.

Disclaimer

Every effort has been made to ensure that the information contained within this guide is accurate at the time of publication. How2Become Ltd is not responsible for anyone failing any part of any selection process as a result of the information contained within this guide. How2Become Ltd and their authors cannot accept any responsibility for any errors or omissions within this guide, however caused. No responsibility for loss or damage occasioned by any person acting, or refraining from action, as a result of the material in this publication can be accepted by How2Become Ltd.

The information within this guide does not represent the views of any third party service or organisation.

CONTENTS

INTRODUCTION

INTRODUCTION TO YOUR NEW GUIDE

Welcome to your new guide, *Numerical Reasoning Tests*. This guide is a comprehensive testing book which provides lots of practice questions for basic, intermediate and advanced mathematics.

This guide contains a variety of mathematical questions for anyone who is asked to take a Numerical Reasoning Test.

The key to success for psychometric testing is through practise and preparation. We have provided you with lots of questions in order for you to gain a complete understanding of what you are likely to face in a Numerical Reasoning Test.

It is important that when working through this book, you check your answers at the end of each testing chapter. Knowing where you went wrong, and understanding what you need to do to reach the correct answer, is just as important as getting the correct answer. If you know how to fix your mistakes, you are far more likely to get the answer correct next time.

Good luck and we wish you all the best.

The how2become team

The How2Become Team

STRUCTURE OF THE BOOK

In order to make the most out of your new guide, it is important to understand the structure of the testing book. We have done our utmost to create a guide that is suitable for all mathematical abilities; to assist you in passing any Numerical Reasoning Test.

Your Numerical Reasoning guide has been broken down into three main sections: basic, intermediate, and advanced. This is to ensure your mathematical skills are tested in the best way possible.

This comprehensive Numerical Reasoning guide follows the structure as formulated below:

- **Introduction to Your New Guide**
  - o What is Numerical Reasoning?
  - o Aims and Objectives
  - o What to Expect
  - o Numerical Reasoning Testing Strategies
- **Numerical Reasoning Example Questions**
- **Numerical Prep**
  - o Mental Arithmetic
  - o Warm Up
- **Numerical Reasoning – Basic**
  - o Numerical Reasoning – Basic (Section 1) and (Section 2)
  - o Detailed Answers and Explanations
- **Numerical Reasoning – Intermediate**
  - o Numerical Reasoning – Intermediate (Section 1) and (Section 2)
  - o Detailed Answers and Explanations
- **Numerical Reasoning – Advanced**
  - o Numerical Reasoning – Advanced (Section 1) and (Section 2)
  - o Detailed Answers and Explanations
- **A Few Final Words…**

Whilst we do not provide an exact account of what your Numerical Reasoning Test will look like, we do provide an insight into what you can expect in terms of questions. The most important thing you need to understand before sitting any Numerical Reasoning Test, is how to answer the questions.

Fundamentally, our How2Become team have designed this guide to:

- Ensure you are fully prepared for a Numerical Reasoning Test;
- Provide different levels of difficulty: basic, intermediate and advanced;
- Provide detailed answers and explanations for you to fully comprehend how to reach the correct answer;
- Demonstrate sample questions, providing a step-by-step account of what you need to do in that particular arithmetic.

WHO TAKES A NUMERICAL REASONING TEST?

A Numerical Reasoning Test is often used in job selection processes to determine whether or not you are suitable for the job role. Numerical Reasoning Tests are a useful way for employers to screen potential employees. This is a great way for them to assess a person's skillset before inviting them back for an interview.

This test will measure your ability to solve mathematical problems and equations. Through practice and perseverance, we will ensure that by the end of the book, you have the knowledge and understanding to answer questions at an array of difficulty levels.

WHAT ARE NUMERICAL REASONING TESTS?

A Numerical Reasoning Test is designed to assess mathematical knowledge through number-related assessments. These assessments can be of different difficulty levels, and will all vary depending on who you are sitting the test for. So, be sure to find out what type of Numerical Reasoning Test you will be sitting, to ensure you are fully able to practice prior to the assessment.

The majority of Numerical Reasoning Tests are administered to candidates who are applying for managerial, graduate or professional positions; any job that deals with making inferences in relation to statistical, financial or numerical data. However, some employers may use these tests as a way of determining important job-related skills such as time management and problem solving efficiency.

Numerical Reasoning Tests cover a wide range of mathematical formulas; and so it is imperative to comprehend the skills and knowledge required to work out the mathematics involved. Most Numerical Reasoning Tests contain questions in relation to:

Adding	Subtracting	Dividing	Multiplying
Fractions	Percentages	Decimals	Ratios
Charts and Graphs	Mean, Mode, Median, Range	Areas and Perimeters	Number Sequences
Time	Conversions	Measure-ments	Money
Proportions	Formulae	Data Interpretation	Quantitative Data
Data Analysis	Correlations	Statistics	Shapes

WHAT SKILLS ARE MEASURED?

Obviously, a Numerical Reasoning Test primarily deals with assessing your level of mathematical ability. Other skills that are also measured, and are often assessed include:

- Critical Reasoning;
- Estimations;
- Speed;

- Concentration;
- Analysis;
- Interpretation.

PREPARING FOR A NUMERICAL REASONING TEST

Your performance in a Numerical Reasoning Test can undoubtedly be bettered through practice! Getting to grips with the format of the test, and gaining an insight into the typical questions you are likely to face will only work to your advantage.

The more you practice, the more you will see your performance excel! With any psychometric test, it is important to fully maximise your skills and knowledge prior to your assessment to ensure the best result.

This comprehensive guide will provide you with lots of sample questions, similar to those that will be found on your Numerical Reasoning Test. Our insightful and ultimate preparation guide will allow you to grasp each question type, understand what is expected, and show you how to work out the correct answer.

WHAT TYPES OF NUMERICAL TESTS ARE THERE?

Numerical Reasoning Tests vary in their format, in both types of question and difficulty. However, they all test similar arithmetic. Before taking your actual test, we advise that you research the type of test that you will be required to sit. The key components, which distinguish different Numerical Reasoning Tests; are Format and Difficulty.

Formats:

- Graph and Charts – to interpret and analyse data and answer the following questions in relation to that data.
- Word Problems – short word problems or passages that deal with riddles and/or calculations.
- Number Sequences – the ability to find the pattern or correlation amongst a sequence.

- Basic Maths – demonstrate basic arithmetical understanding.

Level of Difficulty:

- Basic – Basic GCSE Maths – simple mathematical formulas and calculations, interpretation, analysis.
- Intermediate – Strong GCSE Maths – interpretation, equations, charts and graphs, statistics.
- Advanced – Higher Level Maths – critical reasoning and analysis, quantitative reasoning.

Levels of difficulty and different formats are determined by the job for which you are applying. Your test will solely depend on the nature of the job and the position you are applying for, and therefore the requirements for each test and desired level of ability, will vary.

NUMERICAL REASONING STRATEGIES

- Questions will often require you to identify what mathematical formulae is being used (division, percentage, ratio, etc.). Before you answer the question, carefully read what the question is asking you to do! Be sure to understand what you need to work out, before attempting to answer the question.

- Do not spend too much time on one particular question. You may find some questions easier than others. You may struggle at a certain 'type' of question. It is important not to ponder over questions you are unsure of. If you're able to, move on and then come back to those questions at the end.

- Accuracy is key; avoid silly mistakes! You need to remain as accurate as possible to ensure a high and successful score. That's why it is important to fully comprehend the questions and understand what is being asked.

- These tests are designed under strict time limits. Psychometric testing is fundamentally used to measure people's level of accuracy, whilst working in speedy conditions.

- Working out mental arithmetic can be difficult. Do not be afraid to write down your calculations.

- Practice is key. The more you practice your mental arithmetic and other mathematical formulae; the easier it becomes. This is why we have provided you with lots of sample questions to work through. The more you practice these tests, the more likely you are to feel comfortable and confident with the questions. Remember, practice makes perfect!

- If you are unsure about the answers, make sure you use our detailed answers and explanations to understand how to reach the correct answer. Remember, knowing where you went wrong is just as important as getting the questions correct. Try practising the question again after reading through the answers and explanations to ensure you know where you went wrong.

- Our guide is broken down into three main sections: basic, intermediate and advanced. If you find one testing section relatively easy, maybe try the next level of difficulty. The more you test yourself and your ability, the more confident you will feel when it comes to tackling a numerical test – no matter what level of difficulty it is!

TIPS FOR PASSING NUMERICAL REASONING

Practice!

- No great accomplishment comes easy! You have to work hard at it! Perseverance and practice are two important things to remember when sitting a Numerical Reasoning Test. Nothing will boost your chances at success more than if you practice them prior to your assessment. Not only will this provide clarity and understanding of what to expect, but it will also take off some of the pressure you may be feeling before that all important test!

Stay calm.

- If you lose focus or become overwhelmed during your Numerical Reasoning Test, it is highly likely that this will impact your overall performance. Try to stay calm and focused throughout your assessment. Remember, if you practice prior to the test, you will have far more experience and knowledge going into the test itself, and this is invaluable when comparing your results with others who did not practice, or had no knowledge of the paper beforehand.

You can always work backwards!

- If you get stuck, why not try the sequence in reverse? This will allow you to visualise the sequence from a different perspective; and allow you to spot something you may have missed previously.

Manage your time.

- The time you are allowed to complete your Numerical Reasoning Test will very much depend on your circumstances. Try to find out how long your test is going to last, and use this information to your advantage. Managing your time in psychometric tests is significant; practising these tests prior to your assessment will give you some indication of how well you will perform under extreme time restrictions.

Finally, we have also provided you with some additional free online psychometric tests which will help to further improve your competence in this particular testing area. To gain access, simply go to:

www.MyPsychometricTests.co.uk

Good luck and best wishes,

The how2become team

The How2Become Team

EXAMPLE NUMERICAL REASONING QUESTIONS

Adding Fractions

$$\frac{5}{7} + \frac{3}{5}$$

$$\frac{5}{7} \times \frac{3}{5} = \frac{25 + 21}{35} = \frac{46}{35} = 1\frac{11}{35}$$

Crossbow Method:

The CROSS looks like a multiplication sign and it tells you which numbers to multiply together.

One arm is saying 'multiply the 5 by the 5', and the other arm is saying 'multiply the 7 by the 3'.

The BOW says 'multiply the 7 by the 5'.

The answer is 35 and it goes **underneath** the line in the answer.

Subtracting Fractions

$$\frac{4}{7} - \frac{2}{5}$$

$$\frac{4}{7} \times \frac{2}{5} = \frac{20 - 14}{35} = \frac{6}{35}$$

To subtract fractions, the method is exactly the same. The only difference is, you minus the two numbers forming the top of the fraction, as opposed to adding them.

Multiplying Fractions

$$\frac{2}{3} \times \frac{4}{7}$$

$$\frac{2}{3} \times \frac{4}{7} = \frac{8}{21}$$

Arrow Method:

Multiplying fractions is easy. Draw an arrow through the two top numbers and the two bottom numbers (as shown above) and then multiply – simple!

Sometimes the fraction can be simplified, but in the above example, the answer is already in its simplest form.

Drawing the arrows is just to help you remember which numbers to multiply. Once you have mastered this knowledge, try doing it without the arrows.

Dividing Fractions

$$\frac{3}{7} \div \frac{1}{3}$$

$$\frac{3}{7} \div \frac{3}{1} = \frac{3}{7} \times \frac{3}{1} = \frac{9}{7} = 1\frac{2}{7}$$

Most people think that dividing fractions is difficult. However, it's actually relatively simple if you have mastered multiplying fractions.

Mathematicians realised that if you turn the second fraction upside down (like in the above example), and then change the 'divide' sum to a 'multiply', you will get the correct answer.

Simplifying Fractions

$$\frac{24}{30} = \frac{12}{15} = \frac{4}{5}$$

Simplifying Fractions:

There are a few steps to follow in order to correctly simplify fractions.

- Can both numbers be divided by 2? If yes, then how many times does 2 go into each number? Write the new fraction.

- Using the new fraction, do the same thing. Can 2 go into both numbers? If yes, divide both numbers by 2.

- If both numbers cannot be divided by 2, then try the first odd number: 3. Can both numbers be divided by 3? If yes, divide both numbers by 3. Do this again until 3 no longer goes into the number.

- If 3 does not go into the numbers again, it doesn't mean it's finished. Try the next odd number: 5, and so on until the fraction can no longer be simplified.

Fractions and Numbers

What is $\frac{3}{7}$ of 700?

How to work it out:

- $700 \div 7 \times 3 = 300$.

OR

- $3 \div 7 \times 100 = 300$.

Percentages

What is 45% of 500?

How to work it out:

- To work out percentages, divide the whole number by 100 and then multiply the percentage you want to find.

- **For example:**

  o 500 ÷ 100 x 45 = 225

  o So, 225 is 45% of 500.

Fractions / Decimals / Percentages

$$\frac{1}{10} = 0.1 = 10\%$$

How to turn fractions into decimals, and decimals into percentages:

- To change 0.1 into a percentage, you would move the decimal point two places to the right, so it becomes 10%.

- To convert $\frac{1}{10}$ into a decimal, you would divide both numbers. For example, 1 ÷ 10 = 0.1.

- To convert 10% into a decimal, you move the decimal point two places to the left. For example, to convert 10% into a decimal, the decimal point moves two spaces to the left to become 0.1.

Volume

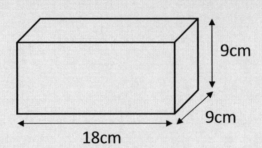

9cm

9cm

18cm

Volume:

Length x base x height

- **18 x 9 x 9 = 1,458**

Areas / Perimeters

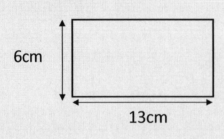

6cm

13cm

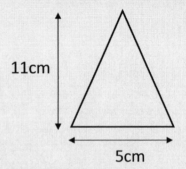

11cm

5cm

Area of squares and rectangles:

Base x height

Area of triangles:

½ base x height

- 11 x 5 ÷ 2 = 27.5 cm

Perimeter:

Add all the sizes of each side.

- 6 + 6 + 13 + 13 = 38 cm

Angles

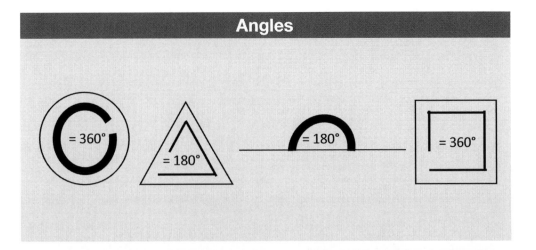

Symmetry

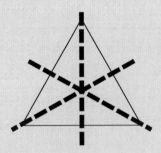

How to work it out:

- To work out how many lines of symmetry a shape has, you need to see where the shape can be folded, in order to create the same reflection.

- Note, an equilateral triangle has 3 lines of symmetry because it can be rotated 3 turns. The triangle would look exactly the same for each rotation.

- **Remember, don't count the same line of symmetry more than once!**

Inputs and Outputs

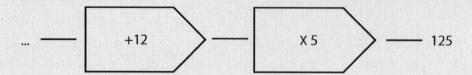

How to work it out:

In order to work out the missing number at the start of the sequence, you will need to work backwards.

- When working backwards, you need to do the OPPOSITE.
- For example:
  - o $125 \div 5 - 12 = 13$
- You can factor '13' into the equation to make sure you have the correct answer, and the equation works.

Simplifying Equations

Simplify 5w - 6x - 2w - 1x

(5w) (- 6x) (- 2w) (- 1x)

(5w - 2w) = 3w

(-6x - 1x) = -7x

3w -7x

- The important thing to remember for simplifying equations is to break up the equation (like above).
- The '-' signs and the '+' signs should also be grouped and be on the left side of the number.

Number Sequences

$$13, 26, 52, 104, 208, 416, ... , ...$$

How to work it out:

In order to work out number sequences, you need to understand what is happening from one number to the next.

- For example, in the above number sequence: you should be able to see the pattern of 'doubling'.
- So, the next number after 416 should be double: 832.
- The next number after 832 should be double: 1664.

Ratios

Ben has some sweets. He is going to share them with his two friends. Ben has 24 sweets and is going to share them in the ratio of 4 : 2 : 2.

How many sweets does each person get?

- Add up the ratios = 4 + 2 + 2 = 8.
- 24 ÷ 8 = 3.
- So, 3 x 4 = 12.
- 3 x 2 = 6.
- 3 x 2 = 6.

So one person will have 12 sweets and the two other people will get 6 sweets.

Prime Numbers

2	3	5	7	11	13	17	19
23	29	31	37	41	43	47	53
59	61	67	71	73	79	83	89

A prime number is a number that can only be divided by 1 and itself.

- For example, no other numbers apart from 1 and 5 will go into 5.

Factors

Factors are numbers that can be divided into the original number. For example, 6 has the factors of 1 and 6, 2 and 3.

Factors of 12:

- Factors are all the numbers that can go into the number.

So, $1 \times 12 = 12$
2×6
3×4

So in ascending order, 1, 2, 3, 4, 6 and 12 are all factors of the number 12.

Multiples

- A multiple is a number which is made from multiplying a number in the same pattern.
- For example, the multiples of 2 are: 2, 4, 6, 8, 10, 12, 14 etc.
- Multiples of 15 are: 15, 30, 45, 60, 75 etc.

Speed / Distance / Time

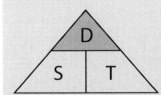 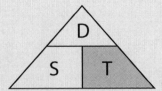 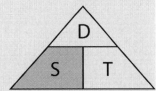

To work out the Distance:

• Distance = Speed x Time

To work out the Time:

• Time = Distance ÷ Speed

To work out the Speed:

• Speed = Distance ÷ Time

Tenths / Hundredths / Thousandths

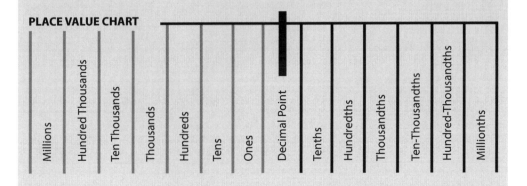

PLACE VALUE CHART

Millions | Hundred Thousands | Ten Thousands | Thousands | Hundreds | Tens | Ones | Decimal Point | Tenths | Hundredths | Thousandths | Ten-Thousandths | Hundred-Thousandths | Millionths

Stem and Leaf Diagrams

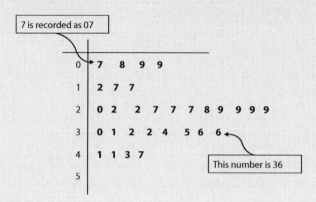

7 is recorded as 07

0	7 8 9 9
1	2 7 7
2	0 2 2 7 7 7 8 9 9 9 9
3	0 1 2 2 4 5 6 6
4	1 1 3 7
5	

This number is 36

- Stem and leaf diagrams act as a way of handling data.
- These become particularly useful when dealing with large sums of data.
- They are also helpful ways to work out the **mean**, **mode**, **median** and **range**.

Mean / Mode / Median / Range

Mean

- To work out the mean of a set of data, you add up all the numbers and then divide the total value by the total amount of numbers.

Mode

- The mode is easily remembered by referring to it as the 'most'. What number occurs most throughout the data?

Median

- Once the data is in ascending order, you can then work out what number is the median. In other words, what number is in the middle? If no number is in the middle, use the two numbers that are both in the middle; add them up and divide by 2.

Range

- In ascending order, the range is from the smallest number to the biggest number.

Percentage Increase

To work out the percentage increase of a set of data, you need to remember this formula:

Percent Increase % = Increase ÷ original number x 100

If your answer is a negative number, then this is a percentage **decrease**.

Percentage Decrease

To work out the percentage decrease of a set of data, you need to remember this formula:

Percent Decrease % = Decrease ÷ original number x 100

If your answer is a negative number, then this is a percentage **increase**.

Mass / Density / Volume

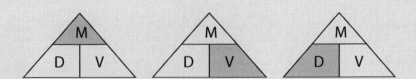

To work out the Mass:

- Mass = Density x Volume

To work out the Volume:

- Volume = Mass ÷ Density

To work out the Density:

- Density = Mass ÷ Volume

Box and Whisker Plots

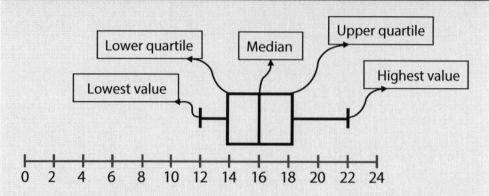

- From the above box and whisker plot, the value of each are as follows:

    o Lowest value = 12

    o Lowest quartile = 14

    o Median = 16

    o Upper quartile = 18

    o Highest value = 22

- The use of box and whisker plots are to help evaluate a set of data and determine the range and quartiles of information.

Hectares

Work out the area of the shape. Write your answer in hectares.

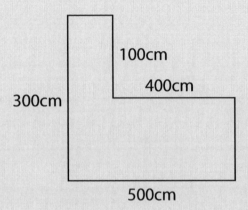

Hectares

The important thing to remember when dealing with hectares, is to use this information as a guideline:

1 hectare = 10,000 m = 2.47 acres

So, if you had measurements in centimetres, you would need to convert them into metres before attempting to convert the measurements into hectares.

Example

For the above example, to work out the area of the shape in hectares, you need to work out the area of the shape first, and then convert the centimetres into metres.

Step 1 = 300 x 500 = 150,000 cm = 150,000 ÷ 100 = 1,500m

Step 2 = 100 x 400 = 40,000 cm = 40,000 ÷ 100 = 400m

Step 3 = 1500 – 400 = 1,100m

Step 4 = to convert 1,100m^2 into hectares, we know 10,000 m^2 = 1 hectare. So, 1,100 ÷ 10,000 = 0.11 hectares.

Velocity Graphs

How much greater is the acceleration of Car B than the acceleration of Car A?

You need to remember this formula:

Acceleration (m/s²) = Change in velocity (m/s²) ÷ Change in time (s)

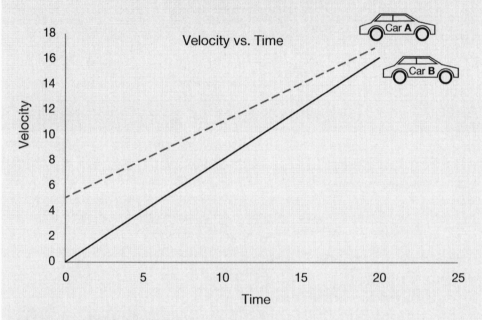

How to work it out:

Step 1 = Car A = change in velocity = 16 – 5 = 11

11 ÷ 20 = 0.55

Step 2 = Car B = change in velocity = 15 – 0 = 15

15 ÷ 20 = 0.75

Step 3 = difference from Car B to Car A = 0.75 – 0.55 = 0.2

Equation Correspondence

A square field, S, has an area greater than 5000m². Its length is decreased by 20m and its width also decreases by 20m to give a rectangular field, R. Which one of the following is true?

A. Perimeter R = area R and perimeter S > area S
B. Area R < area S and perimeter S = perimeter R
C. Area S > area R and perimeter S > perimeter R
D. Area S = area R and perimeter S < perimeter R
E. Area S < area R and perimeter S < perimeter R

Answer = C

How to work it out

- You need to know what '<' '>' and '=' mean in order to work these out.
- '<' means a small number followed by a large number.
- '>' means a large number followed by a small number.
- '=' means the two numbers are equal.

Powers

4^{11}.

- This does not mean 4 x 11.
- 4^{11} means = 4 x 4 x 4 x 4 x 4 x 4 x 4 x 4 x 4 x 4 x 4 = 4,194,304

Gradients

Negative gradients

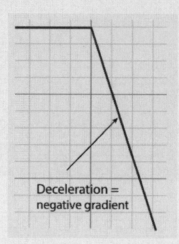

Deceleration =
negative gradient

The negative gradient of a graph is the line that is going downwards (not upwards), if the gradient was going upwards,

Exchange Rate

- If you had to exchange £200 into euros which had the exchange rate of 1.1.46, you would multiply how much you want to exchange (£200) by the exchange rate (1.46).
- So, 200 x 1.46 = 292 euros.

Compound Interest

Compound Interest

If the question is asking you to work out the compound interest, this means that "interest is added on to the interest".

For example, if you financed a car and had to pay 4.6% interest per year for 3 years, including compound interest, based on the rate of £560.

- 560 ÷ 100 x 104.6 = 585.76
- You then use this sum (585.76) to work out the next interest rate.
- 585.76 ÷ 100 x 104.6 = 612.70.
- For the third year, 612.70 ÷ 100 x 104.6 = 640.88.

Water Level Rises

If you were given the question:

30 men take a dip in a swimming pool 40m long and 30m broad. If the average displacement of water by a man is 4m³, what will the rise in the water level be?

How to work it out:

- Total volume of water displaced = 4m³ x 30 (men) = 120m³.
- Rise in water level = 120 ÷ (40 x 30) = 120 ÷ 1200 = 0.1m x 100 = 10cm.
- So, the rise in water level would be 10cm.

NUMERICAL PREP

(MENTAL ARITHMETIC)

Before you begin undergoing numerical questions, the best preparation is to ensure your maths is up to par!

That is why we have provided you with 30 simple mental arithmetic questions. These questions should be be worked out in your head and **WITHOUT** the use of a calculator.

The aim of this section is to just get your mind in gear with some of the basic mathematical concepts.

During this section, you will need to familarise yourself with the following:

- Addition;
- Subtraction;
- Multiplication;
- Division;
- Percentages;
- Decimals;
- Fractions;
- Money.

Question 1

12 x 4

Question 2

329 + 234

Question 3

10% of 1,000

Question 4

500 ÷ 4

Question 5

$^3/_4$ of 60

Question 6

£5.34 + 169p

Question 7

30 x 5

```



```

Question 8

25% of 250

```



```

Question 9

43,234 - 1,495

```



```

Question 10

23.5 + 5

```



```

Question 11

42.4 + 234.7

```



```

Question 12

£3.47 + £83.43

```



```

Question 13

$288 \div 4$

Question 14

40% of £900

Question 15

$^3/_5$ of 700

Question 16

18 x 3

Question 17

50 x 8

Question 18

429,485 + 3.586

Question 19

75 x 5

Question 20

0.45 + 13.6

Question 21

$\frac{1}{5}$ of 25,000

Question 22

82 + 45 + 19

Question 23

5,000 - 82

Question 24

$\frac{3}{4}$ of 150,000

Question 25

$860 \div 20$

Question 26

£39.47 - £19.04

Question 27

70% of 450

Question 28

$2 \times 2 \times 4$

Question 29

28×2

Question 30

$9 \times 9 + 3$

ANSWERS TO NUMERICAL PREP (MENTAL ARITHMETIC)

Q1. 48

Q2. 563

Q3. 100

Q4. 125

Q5. 45

Q6. £7.03

Q7. 150

Q8. 62.5

Q9. 41,739

Q10. 28.5

Q11. 277.1

Q12. 86.90

Q13. 72

Q14. 360

Q15. 420

Q16. 54

Q17. 400

Q18. 433,071

Q19. 375

Q20. 14.05

Q21. 5,000

Q22. 146

Q23. 4,918

Q24. 112,500

Q25. 43

Q26. £20.43

Q27. 315

Q28. 16

Q29. 56

Q30. 84

NUMERICAL PREP

(WARM UP)

Question 1

A charity arranges a bike race. 120 people take part. $1/_3$ of the people finish the race in under half an hour. How many people did not finish the race in under half an hour?

Answer

Question 2

What is $3/_5$ of 700?

Answer

Question 3

There are 4,000 millilitres of water contained in the jug. If 1 litre is equivalent to 1,000 millilitres, how many litres of water are there?

Answer

Question 4

What is the missing angle?

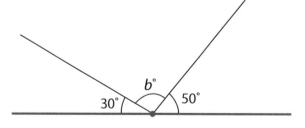

Answer

Question 5

What is 120 multiplied by 13?

Answer

Question 6

Find 60% of £45.

Answer

Question 7

How many lines of symmetry does this shape have?

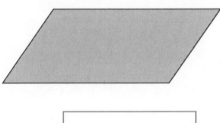

Answer

Question 8

A packet of biscuits weighs 120 g. Find the weight of 9 packets of biscuits.

A	B	C	D
1080 kg	1880 g	1080 g	108 kg

Question 9

A square field has a perimeter of 72cm. What is the area of the square field?

Answer

Question 10

What is $^{24}/_{48}$ in its simplest form?

Answer

Question 11

Look carefully for the pattern, and then choose which pair of numbers comes next.

5   7   9   11   13   15   17 ...   ...

A	B	C	D
18, 19	19, 21	19, 20	21, 23

Question 12

Look carefully for the pattern, and then choose which pair of numbers comes next.

0   1   1   2   3   5   8   ...   ...

A	B	C	D
12, 18	13, 21	15, 23	13, 22

Question 13

Liz has £12.00. Steph has £8.50.

What is the ratio of Liz's money to Steph's money, in its simplest form?

Answer

Question 14

A newspaper includes 16 pages of sport and 8 pages of TV. What is the ratio of sport to TV? Give your answer in its simplest form.

Answer

Question 15

Multiply 6 by 7 and then divide by 3.

Answer

Question 16

Divide 120 by 4 and then multiply it by 5.

Answer

Question 17

What is $9/11$ of 88?

Answer

Question 18

An English class of 28 have just sat a mock Exam. The exam has 2 sections – Literature and Language. It takes approximately 6 minutes to mark the Literature section and 7 minutes to mark the Language section. Another 2 minutes is given on each exam to check the work again. How long in hours and minutes does it take to mark the English mock exam?

A	B	C	D
6 hours and 45 minutes	5 hours and 25 minutes	7 hours	9 hours and 10 minutes

Question 19

What is 0.9 as a percentage?

A	B	C	D
0.009%	0.9%	9%	90%

Question 20

Simplify $x + 8x - 3x$.

A	B	C	D
5x	6x	7x	12x

Question 21

Using the rule of BIDMAS, work out $23.7 - 2.5 \times 8$.

Answer [   ]

Question 22

There are 20 buttons in a bag. 12 are red, 5 are green and the rest are white. A button is chosen at random. Work out the probability that it is white.

Answer ⬚

Question 23

On a school trip at least 1 teacher is needed for every 8 students. Work out the minimum number of teachers needed for 138 students.

Answer ⬚

Question 24

Translate the triangle so that point A moves to point B. Draw your translation on the graph.

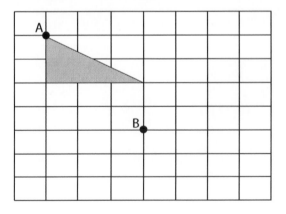

Question 25

Rotate the triangle 90° clockwise so that point A moves to point B. Draw your rotation on the graph.

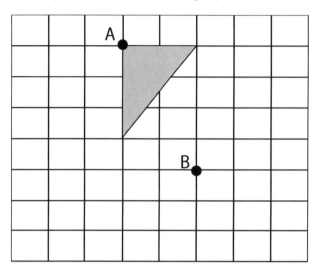

Question 26

The school day starts at 08:45. They have 15 minutes form time and then a 25 minute assembly before the first lesson starts. What time does the first lesson start?

Answer [　　　　　　]

Question 27

A cinema has 27 rows of seats, 28 seats in each row. Tickets are £8 each.

The cinema has sold tickets for every seat apart from 5. Estimate how much, to the nearest hundred, the cinema will make, based on the information provided.

Answer [　　　　　　]

Question 28

How many grams are there in 2.5 kilograms?

A	B	C	D
0.0025g	250g	2005g	2500g

Question 29

What is the value of 9 in 5.92?

A	B	C	D
9/10	1/9	1/90	9/100

Question 30

The scatter graph shows the number of driving lessons and the number of tests taken to pass by 10 people.

What proportion of the 10 people passed on their first test?

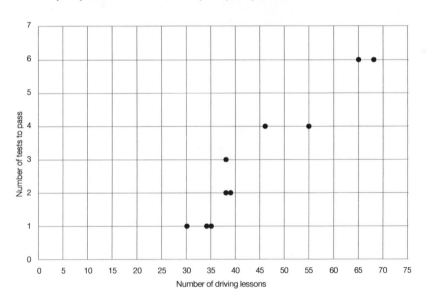

Answer

ANSWERS TO NUMERICAL PREP (WARM UP)

Q1. 80

EXPLANATION = 120 (total number of people) ÷ 3 = 40. This is equal to $\frac{1}{3}$. Therefore: 40 x 2 = 80 (this gives you $\frac{2}{3}$ - which is the number of people who didn't finish the race in under half an hour).

Q2. 420

EXPLANATION = 700 ÷ 5 x 3 = 420.

Q3. 4

EXPLANATION = there are 1,000 millilitres in 1 litre.That means 4,000 millilitres, would be equivalent to 4 litres.

Q4. 100°

EXPLANATION = the angle makes a straight line. A straight line contains angles which add up to 180°.

- So, 180 – 50 – 30 = 100°.

Q5. 1,560

EXPLANATION = 120 x 13 = 1,560.

Q6. £27

EXPLANATION = £45 ÷ 100 x 60 = £27.

Q7. 0

EXPLANATION = this shape is a parallelogram, and these shapes do not contain a line of symmetry. No matter where you draw the reflection line, the shape cannot be reflected symmetrically.

Q8. C = 1,080 g

EXPLANATION = 120 x 9 = 1,080 g. Pay attention to the measurements; the question is in grams (g), so therefore your answer should also be in grams, unless stated otherwise.

Q9. 324 cm²

EXPLANATION = the key thing to remember is that the shape is a square (the sides will be the same length). If the perimeter of the shape is 72 cm, that means 72 needs to be divided by 4 (4 sides). So, 72 ÷ 4 = 18. Each length of the square is 18 cm. To work out the area = 18 x 18 = 324 cm².

Q10. ½

EXPLANATION = $^{24}/_{48}$, both numbers can be divided by 24. It goes into 24 once, and goes into 48 twice. Therefore it gives the fraction of ½.

Q11. B = 19, 21

EXPLANATION = this is a series of repetition. The regular series adds 2 to every number.

Q12. B = 13, 21

EXPLANATION = this is a Fibonacci number sequence. The sequence follows the pattern of adding the two previous numbers together in order to get the next number. For example, the 8 is found by adding the 5 and the 3 together, and so forth.

Q13. 24:17

EXPLANATION = both amounts are in pounds. We have to convert both amounts into pence. £12.00 = 1200p. £8.50 = 850p. Now the ratio is 1200:850. Both sides are divisible by 50. Dividing both sides by 50 gives 24:17. So the ratio is 24:17.

Q14. 2:1

EXPLANATION = the answer is 2:1. You can divide both sides of 16:8 by 8.

Q15. 14

EXPLANATION = 6 x 7 = 42 ÷ 3 = 14.

Q16. 150

EXPLANATION = 120 ÷ 4 = 30 x 5 = 150.

Q17. 72

EXPLANATION = 88 ÷ 11 = 8 x 9 = 72.

Q18. C = 7 hours

EXPLANATION = total time spent marking one exam = 6 minutes (Literature) + 7 minutes (Language) + 2 minutes (checking) = 15 minutes. So, 28 exams will take = 15 (minutes) x 28 (exams) = 420 minutes. Converted into hours and minutes = 7 hours.

Q19. D = 90%

EXPLANATION = 0.9 x 100 = 90%.

Q20. B = 6x

EXPLANATION = x + 8x = 9x. So, 9x – 3x = 6x.

Q21. 3.7

EXPLANATION = this question asks you to use the method of BIDMAS:

- 2.5 x 8 = 20.

- 23.7 – 20 = 3.7

Q22. 3 or $^{3}/_{20}$

EXPLANATION = 20 – 12 – 5 = 3. So your chances of picking a white button is 3 out of a possible 20.

Q23. 18

EXPLANATION = 138 ÷ 8 = 17.25. You need one teacher for every 8 students, therefore you would need 18 members of staff in order to cater for 138 students.

Q24. The correct answer would have to look like this:

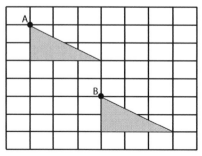

Q25. The correct answer would have to look like this:

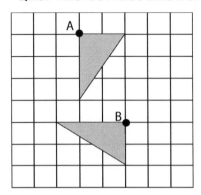

Q26. 09:25

EXPLANATION = 08:45 add 15 minutes (form time) = 9 o'clock. 9 o'clock add 25 minutes (assembly time) = 09:25.

Q27. £6,000

EXPLANATION = 27 rows of 28 seats = 756 – 5 (that are empty) = 751. 751 (number of seats) x £8 = £6,008. To the nearest hundred = £6,000.

Q28. D = 2,500g

EXPLANATION = there are 1,000g in 1 kilogram. Therefore, 2,500g is equivalent to 2.5 kg (2.5 x 1,000 = 2,500g).

Q29. A = $^9/_{10}$

EXPLANATION = we use decimal points to distinguish whole parts from separate parts (tenths, hundredths, thousandths, etc.). A tenth is $^1/_{10}$ of a unit, therefore the 9 represents 9 tenths of part of a unit.

Q30. 30% or $^3/_{10}$ or 0.3

EXPLANATION = the set of data is for 10 people. 3 people passed first time so therefore: 10 ÷ 100 x 3 = 0.3 or 0.3 x 100 = 30% or simply 3 out of 10 ($^3/_{10}$).

NUMERICAL BASIC

(SECTION 1)

Our Numerical Reasoning (basic) section will provide you with the skills and knowledge expected for basic GCSE level mathematics. The difficulty of the questions will depend on the type of Numerical Reasoning Test that you are going to be taking.

In order for you to successfully pass a Numerical Reasoning Test, we have done our utmost to ensure that you have as many questions as possible, that focus specifically on the basics.

In this type of basic Numerical Reasoning Test, you can expect to find questions on the following areas:

- Percentages;
- Fractions;
- Decimals;
- Areas;
- Perimeters;
- Angles;
- Symmetry;
- Inputs and Outputs;
- Data Interpretation;
- Prime, Multiple and Factor Numbers;
- Mean, Mode, Median and Range.

Whilst we have provided you with an array of questions, your Numerical Reasoning Test will be tailored more specifically to the job for which you are applying, and so the questions may not be the same, but will ultimately test the same skills and knowledge in terms of basic arithmetic.

Question 1

Work out $\dfrac{2}{5} + \dfrac{7}{8}$

Answer [   ]

Question 2

Work out $\dfrac{4}{6} \times \dfrac{3}{5}$

Answer [   ]

Question 3

Below is a diagram of a cube. Work out its volume in cubic centimetres.

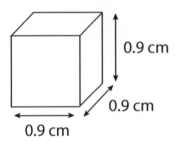

0.9 cm

0.9 cm

0.9 cm

Answer [   ]

Question 4

Three whole numbers add up to a total of 100. The first number is a multiple of 15. The second number is ten times the third number. Both the second and the third number are a multiple of 5. Work out the three numbers.

Answer

Question 5

The probability of picking a lottery winning ticket in the national lottery is 1 in 14 million. If 36 million tickets are sold weekly, how many jackpot winners, on average, would you expect in one week?

A	B	C	D
2,000,000	2	20	1

Question 6

A car travelled 100 metres in 9.63 seconds. On a second occasion, it travelled 200 metres in 19.32 seconds. Which distance had the greater average speed?

A	B	C	D
100 metres	200 metres	Both the same	Cannot say

Question 7

A function is represented by the following machine.

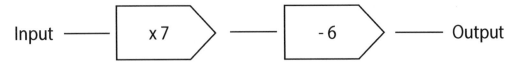

Input ——— x 7 ⟩ ——— - 6 ⟩ ——— Output

A number is put into the machine. The output of the machine is 71. What was the number inputted into the machine?

Answer

Question 8

What is one quarter of 6 hours?

A	B	C	D
1 hour and 30 minutes	95 minutes	180 minutes	1 hour and 20 minutes

Question 9

Simplify $5w - 5x - 4w - 2x$.

Answer

Question 10

A function is represented by the following machine.

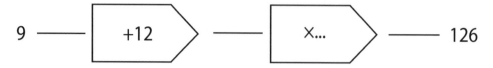

9 is put into the machine. The output of the machine is 126. What is the missing function in the second part of the machine sequence?

Answer [   ]

Question 11

Write down all of the factors of 48.

Answer [   ]

Question 12

What month saw the mode number of pupils to be absent in the one month period, across all five subjects?

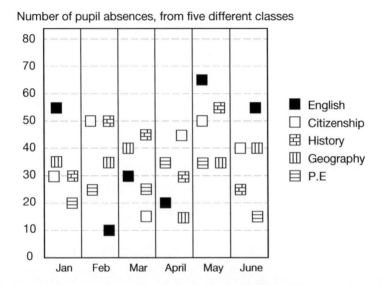

Number of pupil absences, from five different classes

A	B	C	D
February	May	June	March

Question 13

How many different numbers can be made from these four playing cards?

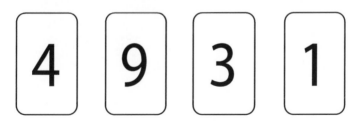

Answer

Question 14

A Science exam is marked out of 50. There are 30 pupils in the class. The marks of the class are as follows:

7	36	41	22	36	22
41	27	29	30	20	17
9	32	47	43	31	29
27	29	32	9	28	35
17	12	8	34	27	29

Using this stem and leaf diagram, add the data in ascending order.

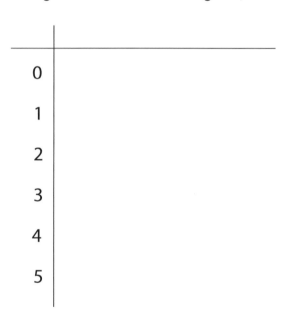

0

1

2

3

4

5

Question 15

Using the above stem and leaf diagram, what is the median?

Answer

Question 16

Work out the angles for A, B and C.

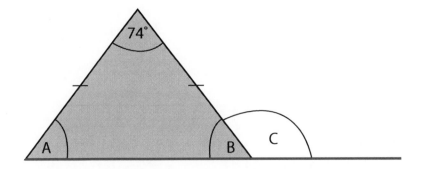

A =

B =

C =

Question 17

Calculate 158 x 67.

Answer

Question 18

A farmer has 630 eggs. They are to be placed in egg trays. Each tray can hold 36 eggs. How many trays will be needed to hold all of the eggs?

Answer

Question 19

Mark is going to make chocolate peanut squares. There are just three ingredients: chocolate, peanut butter, and rice crispies. This is mixed in the ratio 4 : 2 : 3 respectively.

How much of each ingredient will he need to make 900 g of mixture?

Chocolate =

Peanut Butter =

Rice Crispies =

Question 20

Two of the numbers move from Box A to Box B. The total of the numbers in Box B is now four times the total of the numbers in Box A. Which two numbers move?

Box A   **Box B**

2 6		10 1
3		7
9		8
4		5

Answer [ ]

Question 21

Work out 256% of 6,800.

Answer [ ]

Question 22

Subtract $\frac{3}{8}$ of 104 from $\frac{5}{7}$ of 98.

A	B	C	D
27	22	31	41

Question 23

Below is a pie chart illustrating the number of pupils studying a course in the following subject areas.

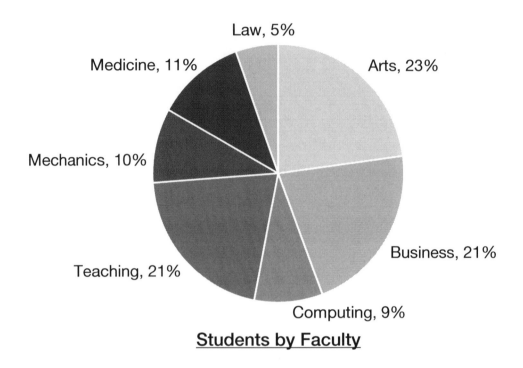

Students by Faculty

If the data is based on 3,620 students, how many of those students are studying either mechanics or law?

Answer [ ]

Question 24

Below is a bar chart displaying some of the heights of the highest mountains.

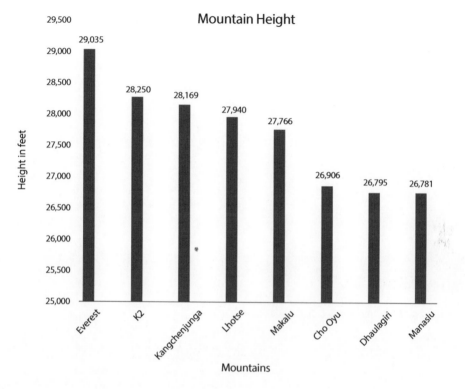

Work out the average height, to the nearest hundred, based on the information provided.

A	B	C	D
27,770	28,000	27,800	27,700

Question 25

Which two numbers come next?

2, 4, 8, 16, 32, 64, ...

A	B	C	D
126 and 215	128 and 256	128 and 265	182 and 265

Question 26

Lisa cycles at an average speed of 8 km/h. How far (in kilometers) does she travel if she cycles for 4 hours?

Answer [　　　　　]

Question 27

James runs from 4.50pm until 5.20pm at an average speed of 7 km/h. How far did he go?

Answer [　　　　　]

Question 28

What is the highest common factor of 12 and 20?

A	B	C	D
4	8	12	2

Question 29

Here is a spinner. Circle the chance of the spinner landing on an odd number.

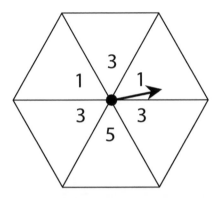

A	B	C	D
$\frac{6}{6}$ or 1	$\frac{4}{6}$	$\frac{1}{2}$	$\frac{1}{3}$

Question 30

What is the angle of D?

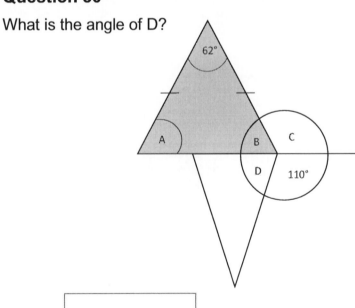

Answer [   ]

ANSWERS TO NUMERICAL REASONING (BASIC SECTION 1)

Q1. $\dfrac{51}{40}$ or $1\dfrac{11}{40}$

EXPLANATION $= \dfrac{2}{5} \times \dfrac{7}{8} = \dfrac{16 + 35}{40} = \dfrac{51}{40}$ or $1\dfrac{11}{40}$

Q2. $\dfrac{12}{30}, \dfrac{6}{15}$ or $\dfrac{2}{5}$

EXPLANATION $= \dfrac{4}{6} \times \dfrac{3}{5} = \dfrac{4 \times 3}{6 \times 5} = \dfrac{12}{30}$ or $\dfrac{6}{15}$ or $\dfrac{2}{5}$

Q3. 0.729 cm³

EXPLANATION $= 0.9 \times 0.9 \times 0.9 = 0.729$ cm³

Q4. 45, 50 and 5

EXPLANATION = three numbers with two of these criteria: a multiple of 15, two numbers in the ratio 10 : 1, and sum of 100.

- Multiples of 15 = 15, 30, 45, 60, 75, 90. So, the first number will be one of these numbers. Two of the numbers follow the rule of: being in the ratio 10 : 1. This works out to be 50 and 5, and will add up to 100 if you add the 45.

Q5. B = 2

EXPLANATION = 36 (million) ÷ 14 (million) = 2.57. So you could expect 2 lottery winners, on average, in a week.

Q6. A = 100 metres

EXPLANATION = 100 ÷ 9.63 = 10.384. 200 ÷ 19.32 = 10.351. Therefore 100 metres has the greatest average speed.

Q7. 11

EXPLANATION = 71 + 6 ÷ 7 = 11. (Remember, to work out the original number, you must work backwards. In order for you to work backwards, you must do the opposite to what the machine is telling you to do).

Q8. A = 1 hour and 30 minutes

EXPLANATION = 6 (hours) x 60 (minutes) = 360 minutes. So, 360 (minutes) ÷ 4 ($\frac{1}{4}$) = 90 minutes.

Q9. 1w – 7x

EXPLANATION = you need to break up the sequence: (5w) (-5x) (-4w) (-2x).

- So, 5w – 4w = 1w and -5x – 2x = -7x. So this simplifies to: 1w – 7x.

Q10. Multiply by 6

EXPLANATION = 9 + 12 = 21. 126 ÷ 21 = 6. Therefore if you put (x6) into the equation (because you divided 126 by 6, you would put the opposite into the equation). Therefore, 9 + 12 x 6 = 126.

Q11. 1 and 48, 2 and 24, 3 and 16, 4 and 12, 6 and 8.

EXPLANATION = the definition of factors is 'all the numbers that can be divided into that number', i.e. what numbers can be multiplied together to reach that number?

Q12. B = May

EXPLANATION = you need to add up all of the subjects for each month. January = 170, February = 170, March = 155, April = 145, May = 240, June = 175. Therefore the mode (the most) in one given month is in May.

Q13. 24

EXPLANATION = starting with the number 4, you can get 6 numbers (4931, 4913, 4319, 4391, 4139, 4193). This can be done for all 4 numbers (if you start with a different number; you will be able to make 6 different numbers). Therefore 6 groups of 4 = 24.

Q14. Your answer should look exactly like this:

0	7	8	9	9							
1	2	7	7								
2	0	2	2	7	7	7	8	9	9	9	9
3	0	1	2	2	4	5	6	6			
4	1	1	3	7							
5											

Q15. 29

EXPLANATION = putting the data in order from smallest to biggest, you then need to find the median (middle) number. Do this by eliminating one number from the start, and one number from the end, until you reach the number in the middle. For this sequence, two numbers are left in the middle: 29 and 29. So, add both numbers and divide it by 2 to find the middle number. So, 29 + 29 ÷ 2 = 29.

Q16. A = 53°, B = 53°, C = 127°

EXPLANATION = a triangle contains 180°. So, 180 - 74° = 106°. Both A and B are going to be the same size (you will notice two small lines placed on both sides of the triangle, illustrating they're the same size and length). So, 106 ÷ 2 = 53°. To work out angle C, a straight line has 180°. You've just worked out angle B is 53°, so 180° − 53° = 127°.

Q17. 10,586

EXPLANATION = first, multiply by 7 (units): 158 x 7 = 1,106. Then add a zero on the right side of the next row. This is because we want to multiply by 60 (6 tens), which is the same as multiplying by 10 and by 6. Now multiply by 6: 158 x 60 = 9,480. Now add the two rows together: 9,480 + 1106 = 10,586.

Q18. 18

EXPLANATION = 630 ÷ 36 = 17.5. So, you would need 18 trays in order to hold all the eggs.

Q19. Chocolate = 400g, Peanut Butter = 200g, Rice Crispies = 300g

EXPLANATION = to work out the chocolate: 900 ÷ 100 x 4 = 400g. To work out the peanut butter = 900 ÷ 100 x 2 = 200g. To work out the rice crispies = 900 ÷ 100 x 3 = 300g.

Q20. 9 and 4

EXPLANATION = if you moved 9 and 4, this leaves Box A with a total of 11. If you add 9 and 4 to 10, 1 7, 8 and 5, you will get 44. Therefore, this is 4 times as many.

Q21. 17,408

EXPLANATION = 6,800 ÷ 100 x 256 = 17,408.

Q22. C = 31

EXPLANATION =

- 104 ÷ 8 x 3 = 39.

- 98 ÷ 7 x 5 = 70.

- So, 70 – 39 = 31.

Q23. 543

EXPLANATION = 3,620 ÷ 100 x 5 = 181 (Law students). 3,620 ÷ 100 x 10 = 362 (Mechanical students). So, the number of law and mechanical students is: 362 + 181 = 543.

Q24. D = 27,700

EXPLANATION = add up all of the sums and divide it by how many mountains there are (8). So, 29,035 + 28,250 + 28,169 + 27,940 + 27,766 + 26,906 + 26,795 + 26,781 = 22,1642 ÷ 8 = 27,705.25. To the nearest hundred = 27,700.

Q25. B = 128 and 256

EXPLANATION = the sequence follows the pattern of 'the power of 2'. In other words, the number is multiplied by 2 each time. So, 64 x 2 = 128 and 128 x 2 = 256.

Q26. 32 km

EXPLANATION = Speed x time. So, 8 x 4 = 32 km.

Q27. 3.5 km

EXPLANATION = the difference between 4.50pm and 5.20pm = 30 minutes. 30 minutes = 0.5 hour. Remember, distance = speed x time. So, distance = 7 x 0.5 = 3.5 km.

Q28. A = 4

EXPLANATION = the factors of 12 are: 1, 2, 3, 4, 6 and 12. The factors of 20 are: 1, 2, 4, 5, 10 and 20. So the highest common factor of 12 and 20 is 4.

Q29. A = $^6/_6$ or 1.

EXPLANATION = the spinner contains only odd numbers. So no matter what number it lands on, you will always spin an odd number.

Q30. 70°

EXPLANATION = 180° − 62° = 118°. So 118° ÷ 2 = 59°. So angles A and B are 59°.

To work out angle C = 180° − 59° = 121°

Then angle D is 360° - 121° - 59° - 110° = 70°

NUMERICAL BASIC

(SECTION 2)

Question 1

Below is a stem and leaf diagram showing the finishing time, in seconds, of 15 sprinters who took part in a race.

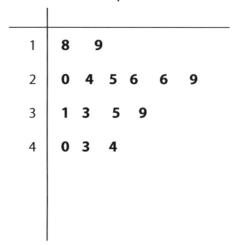

1	8 9
2	0 4 5 6 6 9
3	1 3 5 9
4	0 3 4

What is the median finishing time?

Answer

Question 2

Using the above stem and leaf diagram, what is the mean finishing time? Write your answer to one decimal point.

Answer

Question 3

A ruler is 30 cm in length, correct to the nearest centimetre. What is the smallest possible length of the ruler?

Answer

Question 4

Add $^7/_9$ of 189 to $^5/_8$ of 128.

Answer [   ]

Question 5

Below show three different offers for a 49 inch plasma TV.

Online Store 1

SPECIAL OFFER

Original price =
£268.00

Discount =
20% off!

Online Store 2

SPECIAL OFFER

Original price =
£295.00

Discount =
1/4 off!

Online Store 3

SPECIAL OFFER

Pay £18.50
weekly for 16
weeks

Work out which online store offers the cheapest deal.

Answer [   ]

Question 6

The following table shows the percentage of nickel in two coins.

COIN	WEIGHT	NICKEL
50p coin	8g	25%
20p coin	5g	16%

If both the coins are made of only nickel and copper, what is the difference between the weight of copper present in the 50 pence coin and the weight of copper in the 20 pence coin?

A	B	C	D	E
1.3 g	2.5 g	1.8 g	2 g	3 g

Question 7

How much more does it cost a company to place two 24 x 10 mono advertisements and one 22 x 5 colour advertisements, compared to a company placing three 8 x 10 colour advertisements and one 7 x 5 mono advertisement?

ADVERTISEMENT PRICES		
Size of the Advertisement	Colour	Mono
24 x 10	£12,435	£8,567
22 x 5	£6,437	£4,218
8 x 10	£4,208	£3,987
7 x 5	£2,576	£1,340

A	B	C	D	E
£5,040	£1,365	£10,460	£9,607	£2,464

Question 8

Below is a table representing the actual and target income for 2016 for five different companies.

COMPANY	ACTUAL INCOME (ANNUAL) for 2016	TARGET INCOME (ANNUAL) for 2016
Company A	£234,570	£300,000
Company B	£420,000	£421,560
Company C	£215,750	£450,000
Company D	£310,250	£325,000
Company E	£375,995	£325,000

In the following year, Company B earns £275,000. What is the percentage decrease from Company B's earnings in 2016 and the earnings in the following year? To one decimal place.

A	B	C	D	E
65.5%	45.5%	39.5%	34.5%	41.5%

Question 9

Below is a table representing costs for different products.

PRODUCT	No. of units (1000s)	Cost of material per unit	Manu-facturing costs per unit	Total cost per unit	Sales price per unit	Total Sales Revenue After tax
P	18.5	2.25	2.15	4.4	6.5	38,850
Q	29.5	4.75	2.25	7	10	36,400
R	9	1.5	1.75	3.25	8	42,750
S	13	3.5	2.25	5.75	15	120,250

Product P gets taxed 25% of the total sales revenue. What would the total sales revenue be before tax?

A	B	C	D	E
£43,320	£56,700	£51,800	£52,300	£62,700

Question 10

The table shows the number of times a die was thrown. It shows how many times each number on the die appeared.

Casts	1	2	3	4	5	6
First 10	2	3	1	1	2	1
First 20	5	4	3	4	3	1
First 30	8	5	6	5	4	2
First 40	10	6	7	6	5	6
First 50	13	7	10	7	6	7

The same number did not appear on any two consecutive casts. If the number 4 appeared in the 20th cast, which number/s could not have appeared in the 11th cast?

A	B	C	D	E
4	1	2 and 3	6	3

Question 11

Using the above table, which of the following numbers must have turned up the least amount of times in the first 50 casts?

A	B	C	D	E
2, 4 and 6	6	5	3	1

Question 12

Using the above table, if the same number occurred for the 33rd and the 37th cast, what number/s could it be?

A	B	C	D	E
1	2	4	1 and 6	6

Question 13

A farmland is measured to be 220m in length by 80m in width. What is the approximate area of the field in hectares? 1 hectare = 10,000m^2 = 2.47 acres.

A	B	C	D	E
17 hectares	1.76 hectares	176 hectares	17.6 hectares	7.67 hectares

Question 14

The sterling to US dollar rate is 1:1.32. How many dollars would you receive if you changed up £450?

A	B	C	D	E
$592	$541	$594	$531	$441

Question 15

A flight leaves the airport at 2200 hours. It is an 11 hour and 45 minute flight. There is a 2 hour time difference. What time will they arrive at their destination, assuming the time difference is 2 hours in front?

Answer

Question 16

Multiply 0.04 by 1.1.

Answer

Question 17

What is $^6/_8 \div ^2/_3$? Write your number using mixed fractions and its simplest form.

Answer

Question 18

A lady has been prescribed medication by her doctor. She is prescribed a 10.5 fluid ounce bottle of medication with the instructions to take 0.25 fluid ounces three times a day. How many days does she have to take the medication for?

A	B	C	D	E
7 days	10 days	12 days	13 days	14 days

Question 19

What is $\frac{2}{8}$ x 9?

A	B	C	D
2 1/3	1 1/4	2 2/8	2 1/4

Question 20

Responses when asked how they get to school

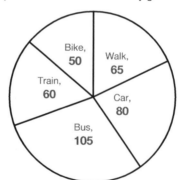

Among the respondents, 80% of the people who said they walk to school and 90% of the people who said they bike to school also said that they used this mode of transport because their school was less than 5 miles away. How many people said that they walk or bike to school because it is less than 5 miles away?

A	B	C	D	E
50	97	120	132	145

Question 21

A History test consists of three papers. The first paper will be marked out of 80, and has a weighting of 35% towards the final grade.

The second paper will be marked out of 60, and has a weighting of 30% towards the final grade.

The third and final test will be marked out of 40, and has a weighting of 35% towards the final grade.

A pupil scores 60 in the first paper, 45 in the second, and 35 in the third paper.

What is the pupil's final percentage score? Give your answer to 1 decimal place.

Answer

Question 22

There are 45 students in a class. 37 students have completed their challenge of reading 6 books. What is the percentage of students who have completed their reading challenge? Round up to the nearest whole number.

Answer

Question 23

Family Tree

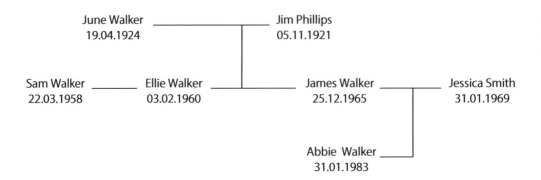

Sam dies before Abbie is born. James was 16 when Sam died. How old was Sam when he died?

A	B	C	D	E
17	23	19	25	28

Question 24

Government spending on "Education services" and "Health services" was 56.3 billion pounds and 106.7 billion respectively for the year 2009-2010. In the same year, the Government spending on "Debt Interests" was 22.22% of the spending on "Education services". The spending on "Education services", "Health services" and "Debt Interests" constituted 50% of the total spending by the Government.

What was the Government's approximate total spending for the year 2009-2010?

A	B	C	D
551 billion pounds	615 billion pounds	351 billion pounds	435 billion pounds

Question 25

STORE	PERCENT CHANGE FROM 2011 TO 2012	PERCENT CHANGE FROM 2012 TO 2013
U	18	-10
V	17	-7
W	16	6
X	20	-5
Y	-15	-8

If the dollar amount of sales at Store W was $456,250 for 2011, what was the dollar amount of sales at that store for 2013?

Answer [   ]

Question 26

Here are four match sticks.

Pattern 1

The pattern continues as follows:

Pattern 1   Pattern 2   Pattern 3

How many match sticks would be in pattern 9?

Answer

Question 27

Below is a table of the total staff at Company A (Staff Distribution).

	HR(%)	Sales(%)	Finance(%)	Media(%)	Distribution(%)	TOTAL(%)
Year 1	21	8	19	32	20	100
Year 2	28	11	17	28	16	100
Year 3	16	21	19	26	18	100
Year 4	13	30	21	14	22	100
Year 5	4	9	25	38	24	100
Year 6	20	27	25	12	16	100

In Year 4, there were 504 people employed in Finance. How many people in total were employed in Year 4 in the department of Sales?

Answer

Question 28

Below is a table listing the percentage changes in earnings from 2012 to 2014 for five different companies.

Company	Percentage Change from 2012-2013	Percentage Change from 2013-2014
Company A	+17%	-5%
Company B	+12%	+5%
Company C	-11%	+8%
Company D	-5%	-7%
Company E	+8%	-3%

At Company E, the amount of sales for 2013, was what percent of the amount of sales for 2014? To one decimal point.

A	B	C	D
3.1%	97.3%	103.1%	115.9%

Question 29

Using the above table, if company B earned £412,500 in 2012, how much money did the company make in 2014?

A	B	C	D
£316,875	£462,000	£415,290	£485,100

Question 30

You are going to drive to your friend's house. She lives 17 miles away from you with an average speed limit of 30mph. Your friend asks for an estimated time of arrival. If you leave your house at 1415, and you stick to the speed limit, what time will you arrive at your friend's house? (Assuming there is no traffic).

A	B	C	D
14:49	15:00	14:32	15:04

ANSWERS TO NUMERICAL REASONING (BASIC SECTION 2)

Q1. 29 seconds

EXPLANATION = 'median' simply means 'middle'. So, what number is in the middle? Using the data in ascending order, you will notice that 29 (seconds) is the median/middle number.

Q2. 30.1 seconds

EXPLANATION = to work out the mean number, add up all the numbers and then divide it by how many numbers there are.

So, 452 ÷ 15 = 30.133. To one decimal point = 30.1.

Q3. 29.5 cm

EXPLANATION = if 29.5 is rounded up to the nearest whole number, it becomes 30cm. If the number is less than 29.5, like 29.4, it would be rounded down to 29 cm. Therefore, 29.5 cm is the smallest possible length the ruler can be.

Q4. 227

EXPLANATION = 189 ÷ 9 x 7 = 147.

• 128 ÷ 8 x 5 = 80.

• So, 80 + 147 = 227.

Q5. Online Store 1 offers the cheapest deal

EXPLANATION = Online Store 1 = 20% off £268.00

• 10% = 26.80

• 20% = 26.80 + 26.80 = 53.60

• 268.00 – 53.60 = £214.40

Online Store 2 = ¼ off £295

• 295 ÷ 4 = 73.75

• 295 – 73.75 = £221.25

Online Store 3 = £18.50 for 16 weeks

• 18.50 x 16 = £296

Therefore Online Store 1 offers the best deal.

Q6. C = 1.8 g

EXPLANATION = to work out the question:

Step 1 = 50p coin = 25% of 8g = 2g (nickel)

= 75% of 8g = 6g (copper)

Step 2 = 20p coin = 16% of 5g = 0.8g (nickel)

= 84% of 5g = 4.2g (copper)

Step 3 = so the difference in copper = 6g – 4.2g = 1.8g

Q7. D = £9,607

EXPLANATION = to work out the question:

Step 1 = first company places orders for two 24 x 10 mono advertisements = 2 x £8,567 = £17,134 and one 22 x 5 colour advertisement = 1 x £6,437 = 6,437

Step 2 = 6,437 + 17,134 = £23,571

Step 3 = second company places orders for three 8 x 10 colour advertisements = 3 x 4,208 = 12,624 and one 7 x 5 mono advertisement = 1 x £1,340 = £1,340

Step 3 = £12,624 + £1,340 = £13,964

Step 4 = difference between the first company and the second company = £23,571 – £13.964 = £9,607

Q8. D = 34.5%

EXPLANATION = 420,000 – 275,000 = 145,000.

• So, 145,000 ÷ 420,000 x 100 = 34.5%.

Q9. C = £51,800

EXPLANATION = 38,850 x 100 = 3,885,000

3,885,000 ÷ 75 = 51,850

Q10. D = 6

EXPLANATION = the question may seem tricky at first, but if you notice, the individual number of 6 was cast once in the first 10 attempts, and only once in the first 20 attempts. Therefore, the number 6 could not have turned up from casts 11 – 20.

Q11. C = 5

EXPLANATION = the number 5 only appears 6 times in the first 50 casts, no other number has a lower cast rate at the end of 50 casts, therefore 5 is the number with the least amount of casts in 50 attempts.

Q12. D = 1 and 6

EXPLANATION = the numbers have to occur more than once between 30 and 40. Only the numbers 1 and 6 do this, therefore this would be the correct answer.

Q13. B = 1.76 hectares

EXPLANATION = 220 x 80 = 17,600 m². 17,600 ÷ 10,000 = 1.76 hectares.

Q14. C = $594

EXPLANATION = in order to work out the exchange rate, you need to multiply the amount (£450) by the exchange rate for which you are changing into ($).

So, 450 x 1.32 = $594.

Q15. 11.45am

EXPLANATION = 10pm + 11 hours 45 minutes = 09.45. Plus 2 hours time difference (ahead) = 11.45am.

Q16. 0.044

EXPLANATION = in order to work out how to multiply decimals, multiply the numbers normally, ignoring the decimal points. Then put the decimal points back into the answer – remember, it will have as many decimal places as the two original numbers combined.

So, 4 x 11 = 44.

To get 4 from 0.04, it has 2 decimal places. To get 11 from 1.1, it has

1 decimal place. Therefore your answer needs to contain 3 decimal places = 0.044.

Q17. 1 $\frac{1}{8}$

EXPLANATION = an easy way to remember how to divide fractions is to turn the last fraction upside down, and then multiply.

So, $\frac{2}{3}$ becomes $\frac{3}{2}$

So, $\frac{6}{8}$ x $\frac{3}{2}$ = 6 x 3 = 18. 8 x 2 = 16. So, we have the fraction = $\frac{18}{16}$

This then needs to be simplified, both numbers can be divided by 2 to make $\frac{9}{8}$.

Finally, we need to change this fraction into a mixed fraction. 8 goes into 9 once, so that is our number before the fraction. We then know 1 is remaining from (9-8), and the number 8 will remain on the bottom of the fraction to form: 1 $\frac{1}{8}$.

Q18. E = 14 days

EXPLANATION = 0.25 x 3 = 0.75 (a day).

So, 10.5 ÷ 0.75 = 14 days.

Q19. D = 2 $\frac{1}{4}$

EXPLANATION = this may seem tricky, but you must remember that '9' is also a fraction. You need to add the 1 underneath it to make $\frac{9}{1}$.

So, $\frac{9}{1}$ x $\frac{2}{8}$ = 9 x 2 = 18 and 1 x 8 = 8. This gives us the fraction = $\frac{18}{8}$. This can be simplified to $\frac{9}{4}$ and as a mixed fraction, is equivalent to = 2 $\frac{1}{4}$.

Q20. B = 97

EXPLANATION = people who walked = 80% of 65 = 65 ÷ 100 x 80 = 52.

People who biked = 90% of 50 = 50 ÷ 100 x 90 = 45. So 52 + 45 = 97.

Q21. 79.4

EXPLANATION = for paper 1 = the score was 60 out of 80 which accounted for 35% of the total mark. So, 60 ÷ 80 x 35 = 26.25.

Paper 2 = 45 ÷ 60 x 30 = 22.5.

Paper 3 = 35 ÷ 40 x 35 = 30.625.

Finally, you need to add up all these percentage scores. So, 30.625 + 22.5 + 26.25 = 79.375.

To one decimal place = 79.4.

Q22. 82%

EXPLANATION = 37 ÷ 45 x 100 = 82.222. To the nearest whole number = 82%.

Q23. B = 23

EXPLANATION = James was 16 = 1965 + 16 = 1981. So Sam died in 1981, 1981 − 1958 = 23.

Q24. C = 351 billion pounds

EXPLANATION = Education services = 56.3 billion pounds and Health services = 106.7 billion pounds.

22.22% of 56.3 = 56.3 ÷ 100 x 22.22 = 12.50986 (Round up = 12.51).

The total of Education, Health and Debt Interests = 175.51 billion pounds.

The total Government spending = 175.51 x 100 ÷ 50 = 351.02.

So, the approximate total = 351 billion pounds.

Q25. $561,005

EXPLANATION = for Store W, in 2011 = $456,250. In order to get from 2011 to 2012, we see a 16% increase. So, 456,250 ÷ 100 x 116(%) = 529,250.

To get from 2012 to 2013, we see a 6% increase. So, 529,250 ÷ 100 x 106 = 561,005.

So, the store amount of sales for Store W in 2013 is $561,005.

Q26. 28

EXPLANATION = In each pattern, the number of match sticks is increasing by 3 each time.

To work out the pattern, you will need to multiply the pattern number by 3 and then add 1.

To work out pattern number 9:

9 x 3 = 27 + 1 = 28

Q27. 720

EXPLANATION = in order to work out the number of people working in Sales in Year 4, you need to work out the total number of employees in that year.

So, 504 (number of people employed in Finance) x 100 ÷ 21 (percentage of Finance) = 2400.

So, 2400 ÷ 100 x 30 (number of employees in Sales) = 720.

Q28. C = 103.1%

EXPLANATION = If A is the dollar amount of sales at Company E for 2013, then 3 percent of A, or 0.03 , A is the amount of decrease from 2013 to 2014. Thus 0.03 = 0.97 (to make a whole one).

Therefore, the desired percent can be obtained by dividing A by 0.97. So, 1 ÷ 0.97 = 1.0309 x 100 = 103.09. Expressed as a percentage to the nearest tenth = 103.1%.

Q29. D = £485,100

EXPLANATION = According to the table, if the dollar amount of sales at Company B was £412,500 for 2012, then it was 12 percent greater for 2013, which is 112 percent of that amount. So, 412,500 ÷ 100 x 112 = 462,000. From 2013 to 2014, the company saw a 5% increase, which is 105% of the previous month. So, 462,000 ÷ 100 x 105 = 485,100. So, the correct answer is £485,100.

Q30. A = 14:49

EXPLANATION = if you travel at an average speed of 30 mph for 17 miles, this will take 34 minutes. If you leave your house at 14:15, you will arrive at 14:49.

NUMERICAL
INTERMEDIATE

(SECTION 1)

Our Numerical Reasoning (intermediate) section will provide you with the skills and knowledge expected for a strong GCSE level mathematical test. The difficulty of the questions will depend on the type of Numerical Reasoning Test you take.

In order to help you pass a Numerical Reasoning Test, we have provided you with lots of questions which will test you on an intermediate level.

In this type of intermediate Numerical Reasoning Test, you can expect to find questions on the following areas:

- Percentages;
- Fractions;
- Decimals;
- Data Interpretation;
- Prime, Multiple and Factor Numbers;
- Mean, Mode, Median and Range;
- Box and Whisker Plots;
- Statistics;
- Currency;
- Mass, Density and Volume;
- Stem and Leaf Diagrams.

Whilst we have provided you an array of questions, your Numerical Reasoning Test will be tailored to the job for which you are applying, and so the questions may not be the same, but will test the same skills and knowledge in terms of an intermediate level numerical test.

Question 1

Representation of the grades students achieved across five subjects

	English	Maths	Science	History	Media	Grade	Pass Mark
David	A-	B+	C-	C+	B+	A+	96-100
Billy	C-	C+	B+	A+	A	A	91-95
Elliott	B+	B-	A+	A-	C	A-	86-90
Taralyn	C+	B+	B+	C+	A+	B+	81-85
Alecia	C	C+	A-	B-	C+	B	76-80
James	B-	B+	C-	C+	C	B-	71-75
Gareth	B+	B-	A	B-	C-	C+	65-70
Duncan	B-	C-	C+	C-	C	C	59-64
Joe	B+	B	B	C	A	C-	50-58

In the above table, find the minimum possible of total marks for all nine candidates in Science.

A	B	C	D	E
507	776	667	676	None of these

Question 2

In the above table, what is the highest mark across all five subjects that David could have got?

A	B	C	D	E
298	386	320	408	None of these

Question 3

There are two lists of numbers. One list contains 11 numbers, the average of which is 36. The second list contains 13 numbers and has the average of 41. If the two lists are combined, what is the average of the numbers in the new list? To the nearest whole number.

A	B	C	D	E
36	37	38	39	40

Question 4

The diagram below shows the plan of a building site. All angles are right angles.

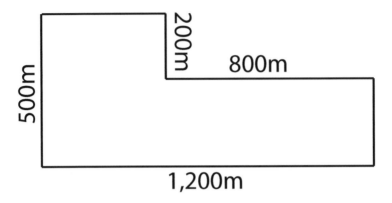

What is the area of the building site? Give your answer in hectares.

1 hectare = 10,000m² = 2.47 acres.

A	B	C	D
60 hectares	40 hectares	44 hectares	4.4 hectares

Question 5

The diagram below shows the layout of an animal sanctuary.

The animal sanctuary contains 6 separate enclosures for different animals.

The animal sanctuary is a rectangle with the following dimensions:

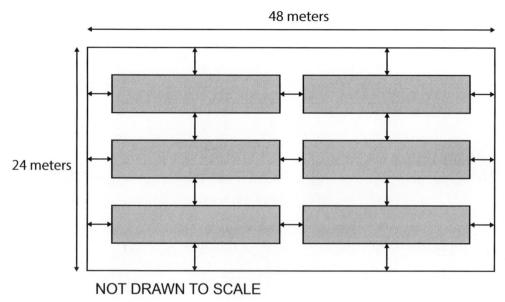

NOT DRAWN TO SCALE

The distance from the outer edge of the sanctuary to the enclosures must be 1.5 metres.

The distance between each enclosure must be 1.5 metres.

Each enclosure is the exact same size. Using the information provided in the diagram above, work out the length and height of an enclosure.

Length

Height

Question 6

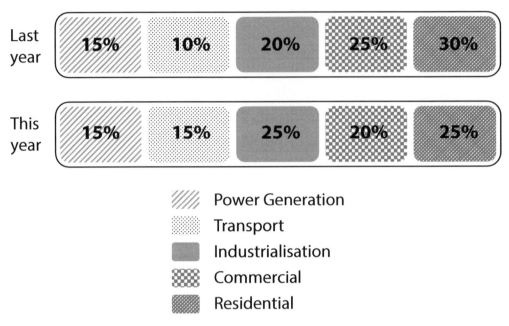

Carbon Emissions

Last year

This year

Power Generation
Transport
Industrialisation
Commercial
Residential

If transport emitted 6 million tons this year, and industrial emissions are the same as last year, what were the commercial emissions last year?

A	B	C	D	E
11.5 million tons	10 million tons	3 million tons	12.5 million tons	8.5 million tons

Question 7

A square field, S, has an area greater than 6400m2. Its length is increased by 31m and its width is also increased by 35m to give a rectangular field, R. Which one out of the following is true?

A. Area S > area R and perimeter S > perimeter R

B. Area S = area R and perimeter S = perimeter R

C. Area S < area R and perimeter S < perimeter R

D. Area S < area R and perimeter S > perimeter R

E. Area S > area R and perimeter S = perimeter R

Answer

Question 8

A bank pays 6.8% compound interest per year on an investment of £7,000.

What is the value of the investment after two years? Round your answer to 2 decimal places.

Answer

Question 9

The following table shows the cost of booking holidays from a travel agent for next year.

HOLIDAY PRICES				
Types of Holiday Deals	Turkey	Mexico	America	Spain
All inclusive	£276pp	£720pp	£880pp	£320pp
Half board	£220pp	£640pp	£795pp	£275pp
Self-Catering	£180pp	£550pp	£620pp	£235pp

Work out the difference in cost of booking three all-inclusive holidays to Mexico, for two people, instead of booking one-self-catering holiday to Turkey for five people.

A	B	C	D
£1,250	£3,420	£9,000	£4,500

Question 10

Kent Police have put out a tender for electrical equipment and supplies. Below are quotes from 3 suppliers.

Electrical Equipment and Supplies	Supplier 1 Total cost over 2 years (£)	Supplier 2 Total cost over 2 years (£)	Supplier 3 Total cost over 1 years (£)
Basic Services	34,550	36,660	15,450
Electrical Safety Checks	39,550	42,000	20,000
Full Equipment Maintenance	120,850	150,500	60,000

Based on an annual year cost, which supplier offers the best price for electrical safety checks?

A	B	C	D
Supplier 1	Supplier 2	Supplier 3	All the same

Question 11

Study the following graph carefully and answer the questions given below.

This graph shows the distribution of candidates who were enrolled for a fitness course and the candidates (out of those enrolled) who passed the course in different institutes.

Candidates enrolled = 1500

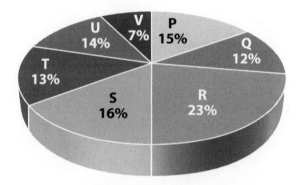

Candidates passed = 920

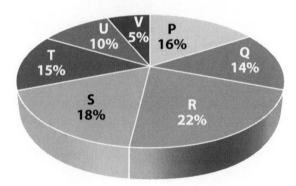

Which institute has the highest percentage of candidates passing the selection process to candidates enrolled?

A	B	C	D
Institute P	Institute Q	Institute T	Institute V

Question 12

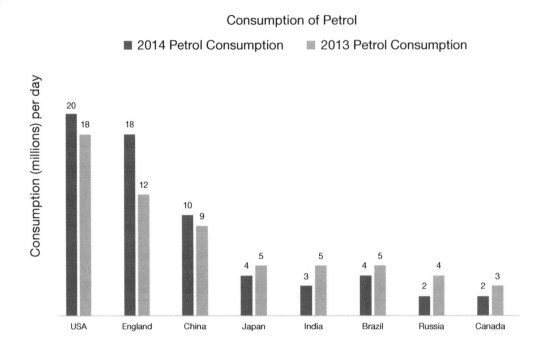

Consumption of Petrol

■ 2014 Petrol Consumption   ■ 2013 Petrol Consumption

In England, if the petrol consumption per year continued to rise by 6.8% until 2016 and then decreased by 4% from 2016 to 2018, what would be the petrol consumption per day in 2018?

A	B	C	D
18.9 million	19 million	21.5 million	19.8 million

Question 13

The set of data below shows the results in a year 11 Media mock exam. The marks are out of 100%. The teacher wants to find the mean mark for this test which was given to 68 pupils. Give your answer to 1 decimal place.

Media mock exam (%)	No. of pupils	No. of pupils X media mock exam (%)
10	0	10 x 0 = 0
20	2	20 x 2 = 40
30	3	
40	6	
50	8	
60	11	
70	8	
80	15	
90	12	
100	3	
Totals	68	

The mean mark is:

Question 14

Look at the sequence below:

1   9   17   25   33   ...   ...

What are the next two terms in the sequence?

Question 15

A sequence uses the following rule:

$$n^{th} \text{ term} = 3(n + 1)$$

Work out the first six terms in this sequence, using the rule provided. 'N' represents the term number in the sequence. Fill in the table below with your answers.

1st term	2nd term	3rd term	4th term	5th term	6th term

Question 16

Factorise:

$$12 + 20x$$

Question 17

Factorise:

$$x^2 - 81$$

Question 18

Solve:

$$6(x - 3) = x + 7$$

Question 19

Simplify:

$$a^2 + a^2$$

Queston 20

Factorise completely:

$$20a^2 - 10a$$

Question 21

(a) Circle the THREE squared numbers.

17   45   49   12   64   91   50   4   5   18   30   15

(b) Circle ALL of the factors of 90.

17   45   49   12   64   91   50   4   5   18   30   15

(c) Circle ALL of the prime numbers.

17   45   49   12   64   91   50   4   5   18   30   15

Question 22

Here is a map of an island.

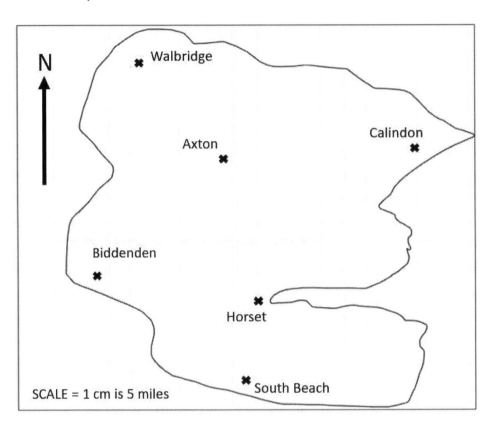

Write down the bearing from Calindon to Biddenden.

Question 23

Write each of the following expressions in their simplest form.

(a) 8^0

(b) $9^9 \times 9^5$

[ ]

(c) $7^8 \div 7^7$

[ ]

(d) $13^9 \div 13^1$

[ ]

(e) $y^{15} \times y^4$

[ ]

Question 24

Using trial and improvement, solve the equation $x^2 + 2x = 40$, correct to 1 decimal place.

[ ]

Question 25

Andy says that 4 x 3 – 2 x 7 = -2

Ryan says the answer to this calculation is 70.

Who is correct, and explain your reasons why.

Question 26

Calculate the following

$$(5.5 \times 10^7) – (3.14 \times 10^4)$$

Give your answer in standard form.

Question 27

The below diagram shows one square and four regular pentagons.

Work out the value of x.

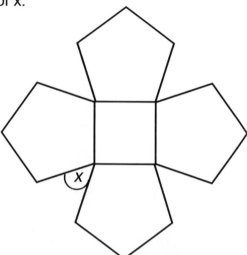

Question 28

The following table lists the type of bonus each member of staff will receive if they reach a specific number of sales per hour they work. The table has not yet been completed. Staff work seven hour shifts. In order to answer the questions, you will need to complete the table.

TIME	10 sales	20 sales	30 sales	40 sales
1st hour	£23.50	£27.50	£35.95	£42.60
2nd hour	£20.00	£23.50	-	£36.35
3rd hour	£16.50	-	£25.55	-
4th hour	£13.00	£15.50	£20.35	-
5th hour	£9.50	-	£15.15	£17.60
6th hour	-	£7.50	£9.95	£11.35
7th hour	£2.50	£3.50	-	£5.10

How much would a worker earn in bonuses if they reached 10 sales during their first and last hour, 20 sales during the 2nd and 6th hours, 30 sales during the 3rd and 5th hours, and 40 sales during the 4th hour?

A	B	C	D
£124.50	£124	£125.55	£121.55

Question 29

Jasmine has two 4-sided dice.

The first dice has the numbers 1, 6, 7 and 9.

The second dice has the numbers 2, 3, 8 and 4.

How many different combinations can be made if both dice are rolled at the same time?

Question 30

On the grid, represent x + y = 4, with values of x from -2 to 4.

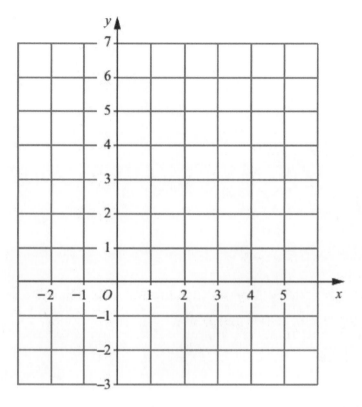

ANSWERS TO NUMERICAL REASONING (INTERMEDIATE SECTION 1)

Q1. D = 676

EXPLANATION = 50 + 81 + 96 + 81 + 86 + 50 + 91 + 65 + 76 = 676.

Q2. E = none

EXPLANATION = 90 + 85 + 58 + 70 + 85 = 388. None of the answers match, so therefore the answer must be 'none'.

Q3. D = 39

EXPLANATION = 11 x 36 = 396. 13 x 41 = 533. 533 + 396 = 929 ÷ (11 + 13) = 38.708. To the nearest whole number = 39.

Q4. C = 44 hectares

EXPLANATION = Work out the area of the whole shape: 1200 x 500 = 600,000

Work out the area of the missing rectangle (to make a complete rectangle): 800 x 200 = 160,000

- So, 600,000 – 160,000 = 440,000m².
- 440,000m² in hectares = 440,000 ÷ 10,000 = 44 hectares.

Q5. Length of each enclosure = 21.75 metres, Height of each enclosure = 6 metres

EXPLANATION = To work out the length = total 48 metres

- 48 – 1.5 – 1.5 – 1.5 = 43.5
- 43.5 ÷ 2 = 21.75 metres

To work out the height = total 24 metres

- 24 – 1.5 – 1.5 – 1.5 – 1.5 = 18
- 18 ÷ 3 = 6 metres

Q6. D = 12.5 million tons

EXPLANATION = if transport emissions this year are 6 million tons – and equal 15% of the total – the overall total for this year would be 6,000,000 x 100 ÷ 15% = 40,000,000.

So industrial emissions for this year would be = 40,000,000 ÷ 100 x 25 = 10,000,000.

The industrial emissions are the same for last year, so to work out the overall total of last year = 10,000,000 x 100 ÷ 20 = 50,000,000.

So the commercial emissions for last year = 50,000,000 ÷ 100 x 25 = 12,500,000 (12.5 million tons).

Q7. C = Area S < area R and perimeter S < perimeter R

EXPLANATION = if the perimeter is increased on both sides of the Square field S, that means the area of square field R is going to be bigger. This is also true about the perimeter; if both sides are increased in size to form field R, which means the perimeter for R is going to be bigger than that of perimeter S. So, the correct way to demonstrate this is answer C.

Q8. £7984.37

EXPLANATION = for this question, it is vitally important to remember that interest will be added on to previous interest.

Step 1 = for the first year = 7,000 ÷ 100 x 6.8 = £476.

- So, 7,000 + 476 = 7,476.

Step 2 = for the second year = 7,476 ÷ 100 x 6.8 = 508.37.

- So, 7,476 + 508.37 = £7984.37.

Q9. B = £3,420

EXPLANATION = Self-catering holiday to Turkey for 5 people = 180 x 5 = 900.

All-inclusive holiday to Mexico for 2 people = 720 x 2 = 1440. Booked three times = 1440 x 3 = 4320.

- So, 4320 – 900 = 3,420.

Q10. A = Supplier 1

EXPLANATION = Supplier 1 = 39,550 ÷ 2 = 19775

Supplier 2 = 42,000 ÷ 2 = 21,000

Supplier 3 = 20,000

Therefore, Supplier 1 offers the best price for electrical safety checks, for one year.

Q11. B = Institute Q

EXPLANATION =

$$P = \left[\left(\frac{16\% \text{ of } 920}{15\% \text{ of } 1500}\right) \times 100\right]\% = \left[\frac{16 \times 920}{15 \times 1500} \times 100\right]\% = 65.42\%.$$

$$Q = \left[\left(\frac{14\% \text{ of } 920}{12\% \text{ of } 1500}\right) \times 100\right]\% = 71.56\%.$$

$$R = \left[\left(\frac{22\% \text{ of } 920}{23\% \text{ of } 1500}\right) \times 100\right]\% = 58.67\%.$$

$$S = \left[\left(\frac{18\% \text{ of } 920}{16\% \text{ of } 1500}\right) \times 100\right]\% = 69\%.$$

$$T = \left[\left(\frac{15\% \text{ of } 920}{13\% \text{ of } 1500}\right) \times 100\right]\% = 70.77\%.$$

$$U = \left[\left(\frac{10\% \text{ of } 920}{14\% \text{ of } 1500}\right) \times 100\right]\% = 43.81\%.$$

$$V = \left[\left(\frac{5\% \text{ of } 920}{7\% \text{ of } 1500}\right) \times 100\right]\% = 43.81\%.$$

So, the institute with the highest percentage rate of candidates passed, to candidates enrolled, is Institute Q.

Q12. A = 18.9 million

EXPLANATION = first, you need to work out the percentage increase each year from 2014 to 2016.

So, in 2014 there is 18 (million); to work out a 6.8% increase would equal 106.8%. So, 18 ÷ 100 x 106.8 = 19.2 (million). This is the consumption for 2015. From 2015 to 2016, the same thing applies. 19.2 ÷ 100 x 106.8% = 20.5 (million).

From 2016 to 2017, there is a 4% decrease. So, 20.5 ÷ 100 x 96% = 19.7 (million). From 2017 to 2018 = 19.7 ÷ 100 x 96% = 18.9 (million).

Q13. 67.2%

EXPLANATION = Add up the "number of pupils multiplied by media mock exam" and then divide it by the "number of pupils".

Media mock exam (%)	No. of pupils	No. of pupils X media mock exam (%)
10	0	10 x 0 = 0
20	2	20 x 2 = 40
30	3	30 x 3 =90
40	6	40 x 6 = 240
50	8	50 x 8 = 400
60	11	60 x 11 = 660
70	8	70 x 8 = 560
80	15	80 x 15 = 1200
90	12	90 x 12 = 1080
100	3	100 x 3 = 300
Totals		

So, 4570 ÷ 68 = 67.2%.

Q14. 41 and 49

EXPLANATION = The number sequence is adding 8 to the previous number.

Q15. Your answer should look like this:

1st term	2nd term	3rd term	4th term	5th term	6th term
6	9	12	15	18	21

Q16. 4 (3 + 5x)

Q17. (x + 9) (x – 9)

Q18. x = 5

- 6x - 18 = x + 7
- 5x - 18 = 7
- 5x = 25
- x = 5

Q19. $2a^2$

- a + a = 2a
- Both of these are being squared, so 2a squared = $2a^2$.

Q20. 10a (2a – 1)

- Highest common factor = 10
- 10a (2a – 1)
- = $20a^2$ - 10a

Q21. (a) 49, 64 and 4

- 2 x 2 = 4
- 7 x 7 = 49
- 8 x 8 = 64

Q21. (b) 45,   5,   18,   30,   15

EXPLANATION = The factors of 90 are:

- 1 and 90;
- 2 and 45;
- 3 and 30;
- 5 and 18;
- 6 and 15;
- 9 and 10.

Q21. (c) 17 and 5

EXPLANATION = Prime numbers are numbers that can only be divided by itself and one:

- 1 x 17 = 17 (no other numbers can be divided into 17).

- 1 x 5 = 5 (no other numbers can be divided into 5).

Q22. 249°

- The bearing from Calindon to Biddenden is 249°.

Q23. (a) 1

Q23. (b) 9^{14}

- $9^9 \times 9^5 = 9^{9+5}$

Q23. (c) 7^1 or 7

- $7^8 \div 7^7 = 7^{8-7}$

Q23. (d) 13^8

- $13^9 \div 13^1 = 13^{9-1}$

Q23 (e) y^{19}

- $y^{15} \times y^4 = y^{15+4}$

Q24. x = 5.4

Let's start with y = 5

- 5 x 5 = 25

- 2 x 5 = 10

- 25 + 10 = 35 TOO SMALL

Let's try with y = 6

- 6 x 6 = 36

- 2 x 6 = 12

- 36 + 12 = 48 TOO BIG

Let's try with y = 5.5

- 5.5 x 5.5 = 30.25

- 2 x 5.5 = 11

- 30.25 + 11 = 41.25 TOO BIG

Let's try with y = 5.4

- 5.4 x 5.4 = 29.16

- 2 x 5.4 = 10.8

- 29.16 + 10.8 = 39.96 CLOSE

Therefore correct to 1 decimal place = 5.4

Q25. Andy is correct. You need to do the multiplications before subtraction (BIDMAS).

- 4 x 3 = 12
- 2 x 7 = 14
- 12 – 14 = -2

Q26. 5.49686×10^7

- 55,000,000 – 31,400
- 54,968,600
- $= 5.49686 \times 10^7$

Q27. 54°

- Angles in a square = 90° (90 x 4 = 360°)
- Angles in a regular pentagon = 108°
- 360 – 108 – 108 – 90 = 54°

Q28. D = £121.55

EXPLANATION = £23.50 + £2.50 + £23.50 + £7.50 + £25.55 + £15.15 + £23.85 = £121.55

Q29. 16

EXPLANATION = There are 16 different combinations. The first set of combinations are: (1, 2) (1, 3) (1, 8) (1, 4).

- That means there are four sets of combinations for each number.

Q30. Your answer should look like this:

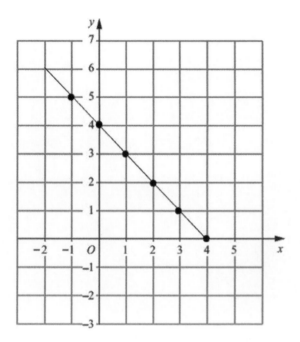

NUMERICAL
INTERMEDIATE

(SECTION 2)

Question 1

Write the following in the form a√b where a and b are integers.

$$\sqrt{38} \times \sqrt{20}$$

Question 2

Work out the mode, median and mean of the following data set:

| 8 | 4 | -4 | -3 | 1 | 4 | 2 | 13 | 9 | 13 | -2 | 4 | 3 |

a) Mode

b) Median

c) Mean

Question 3

Make b the subject of the formula:

$$\sqrt{\frac{b+9}{a}} = 12c$$

Question 4

Evaluate 8^{-4}. Leave your answer in fraction form.

Question 5

In any given week, the probabilities of Andy and Dave playing football are 0.5 and 0.3 respectively. Work out the probability that, in any given week, either Andy plays football, Dave plays football, or both play football.

Question 6

A straight line has a gradient of 4 and a y intercept of 6. Work out the equation of the line.

Question 7

Solve the following linear inequality:

$$2 - 6x \leq -8x - 4$$

Question 8

Fully simplify the following expression:

$$\frac{32a^3b^8}{8ab^4}$$

Question 9

Express the following expression as a single fraction and write this in its simplest form.

$$\frac{2(4y+2)}{8y^2-4} - \frac{2}{4y+1}$$

Question 10

Below is a right-angled triangle.

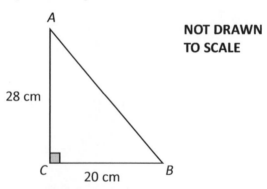

NOT DRAWN
TO SCALE

28 cm

20 cm

A

C

B

Work out the length of side AB. Write your answer to the nearest whole number. You must show ALL of your working out.

Question 11

Find the coordinates of Point Z on the unit circle. Give your answer to 2 decimal places.

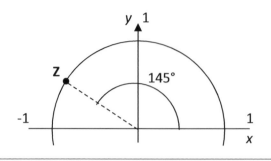

Question 12

Solve the simultaneous equation:

$$y = x^2 + 3 \text{ and } y - 2x = 18$$

Question 13

A square field, S, has an area greater than 2,916 m². Its length is decreased by 14 metres and its width is increased by 14 to give a rectangular field, R.

Which one of the following is true?

A. Area S < Area R and Perimeter S > Perimeter R

B. Area S > Area R and Perimeter S > Perimeter R

C. Area S = Area R and Perimeter S = Perimeter R

D. Area S < Area R and Perimeter S = Perimeter R

E. Area S > Area R and Perimeter S = Perimeter R

Question 14

A field is shown on a map. The field measures 6cm by 8cm on the map and the scale of the map is 1 : 6,000. Given that 10,000m² is equivalent to 1 hectare, what is the area of the field in real life in hectares?

A. 16 hectares

B. 17.28 hectares

C. 19 hectares

D. 20.55 hectares

E. 21 hectares

Question 15

The following graph shows the velocity of two cars at different times.

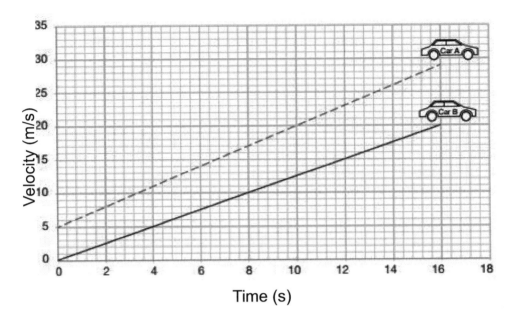

How much greater is the acceleration of Car A than the acceleration of Car B?

Acceleration (m/s²) = Change in velocity (m/s) / Change in time (s)

A. 1.83 m/s²

B. 0.25 m/s²

C. 0.53 m/s²

D. 1.73 m/s²

E. 0.63 m/s²

Question 16

Annual Taxable Income Bracket ($)	Tax Rate	Total Tax paid ($) at the top of this taxable income bracket
0-8,950	10%	895
8,950-36,250	15%	4,990
36,250-87,850	25%	17,890
87,850-183,250	28%	44,602
183,250-400,000	33%	116,129.50
Over 400,000	39.6%	

The table shows the total tax paid in $ on annual taxable income.

For example, a person with an annual taxable income of $60,000 will pay $4,990 plus 25% of ($60,000 - $36,250).

Sam has an annual taxable income of $18,500. The income tax, to the nearest $, he has to pay is:

A. $2,328

B. $2,456

C. $2,139

D. $1,985

E. $3,457

Question 17

The number of people with Malaria in Country A is 80% of the number of people with Malaria in Country B. The number of people with Malaria in Country C is 25% of that in Country A.

If the number of people with Malaria in Country C is 2350, what is the number of people with Malaria in Country B?

A. 10,500

B. 13,750

C. 11,750

D. 11,500

E. 14,550

Question 18

The maximum amounts any family can claim for "Basic Working Tax Credits", "Severe Disability Tax Credits" and "Child Tax Credits" are £1,940, £1,255 and £545 respectively.

Suppose a family is eligible to claim 70% of the maximum tax credits in each category. What is the total amount of tax credits the family can claim?

A	B	C	D	E
£2,618	£3,119	£2,186	£1,628	£1,268

Question 19

Kent Police have put out a notice for staff to enrol onto training courses. Below are quotes from 3 suppliers.

Academic training course	College 1 Total cost over 4 years (£)	College 2 Total cost over 2 years (£)	College 3 Total cost over 6 years (£)
PR and Advertising	14,500	8,350	34,500
Finances	18,250	8,750	42,750
Social Media	24,050	13,000	72,000

What percentage of the total quote provided by College 2 accounts for Social Media training?

A	B	C	D
40.1%	45.6%	43.2%	44.5%

Question 20

Place the numbers from 1 to 9 in each square. Each number should only be used once. The number in the circle should equal the sum of the four surrounding squares. Pay attention to the colour of the squares. Each colour needs to represent the total as shown in the coloured circles underneath the grid.

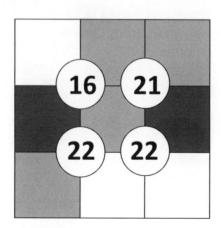

ANSWERS TO NUMERICAL REASONING (INTERMEDIATE SECTION 2)

Q1. $2\sqrt{190}$

EXPLANATION = $\sqrt{38} \times \sqrt{20} = \sqrt{(38 \times 20)} = \sqrt{760}$

However when simplifying surds you are often asked to go a step further by looking for square factors. In this example 760 has a factor of 4 because 4 × 190 = 760. We can now write that $\sqrt{760} = \sqrt{(4 \times 190)} = \sqrt{4} \times \sqrt{190}$.

Now because $\sqrt{4} = 2$, so we can rewrite this again: $\sqrt{4} \times \sqrt{190} = 2\sqrt{190}$.

Q2.

a) 4

* The number that occurs the most number of times is 4.

b) 4

* If you put all the numbers in ascending order, and find the 'middle' number, you will reach the answer of 4.

c) 4

* To work out the mean, you need to add up all of the numbers, and then divide it by how many numbers there are.

* 52 ÷ 13 = 4

Q3. b = 144ac² - 9

EXPLANATION = step 1 = square both sides to get rid of the square root = $(b + 9) \div a = (12c)^2$

Step 2 = Multiply by a to get rid of the fraction = $b + 9 = 144ac^2$

Step 3 = Collect all the terms without b on the right-hand side by subtracting 9:

$b = 144ac^2 - 9$

Q4. $\dfrac{1}{4{,}096}$

EXPLANATION = $8^{-4} = \dfrac{1}{8^4} = \dfrac{1}{4{,}096}$

Q5. 0.65

EXPLANATION = P("Andy plays OR Dave plays") = 0.5 + 0.3 - 0.15 = 0.65.

So, P(A or D) = 0.5 + 0.3 − 0.15 = 0.65

Q6. y = 4x + 6

EXPLANATION = the gradient is 4, and the y-intercept is 6.

So, y = 4x + 6

Q7. x ≤ -3

EXPLANATION = 2 − 6x ≤ -8x − 4 so 2x ≤ -6 so x ≤ -3

Q8. $4a^2b^4$

EXPLANATION = first, divide the numbers: 32 ÷ 8 = 4 = $\dfrac{4a^3b^8}{ab^4}$

Next, cancel the common factor a: $\dfrac{4a^2b^8}{b^4}$

Apply exponent rule: $x^a \div x^b = x^{a-b}$

$b^8 \div b^4 = b^{8-4} = b^4$

So the answer is $4a^2b^4$

Q9.
$$\frac{4y2+6y+3}{8y3+2y2-4y-1}$$

EXPLANATION =

$$\frac{2(4y+2)}{8y2-4} - \frac{2}{4y+1}$$

$$= \frac{16y2+24y+12}{32y3+8y2-16y-4}$$

$$= \frac{4y2+6y+3}{8y3+2y2-4y-1}$$

Q10.34 cm

EXPLANATION = ACB = right angle

AC = 28 cm

BC = 20 cm

AB² = 28² + 20²

= 784 + 400 = 1,184

= √1,184 = 34.4093…

To the nearest whole number = 34 cm.

Q11. (-0.82, 0.57)

EXPLANATION = Point Z is on the unit circle.

The x coordinate is cos 145° = -0.81915…

The y coordinate is sin 145° = 0.57357…

So, the coordinates of Point Z to 2 d.p. are (-0.82, 0.57)

Q12. x = -3 and y = 12 OR x = 5 and y = 28

Q13. E

EXPLANATION = the area of S will be larger than the area of R. The perimeter of S and R will remain the same.

Q14. B

Q15. B

Q16. A

Q17. C

Q18. A

Q19. C = 43.2%

EXPLANATION = 13,000 + 8,750 + 8,350 = 30,100

13,000 ÷ 30,100 x 100 = 43.18%

Rounded to 43.2%

Q20.

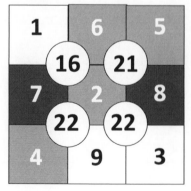

NUMERICAL
ADVANCED

(SECTION 1)

Our advanced Numerical Reasoning section will provide you with the skills and knowledge you will be expected to demonstrate when taking a paper that contains particularly challenging mathematical questions. The difficulty of the questions will depend on the type of Numerical Reasoning test you take.

In order for you to successfully pass a Numerical Reasoning Test, we have done our utmost to ensure you with lots of questions that focus specifically on an advanced level.

In this type of advanced Numerical Reasoning Test, you can expect to find questions on the following areas:

- Percentages;
- Fractions;
- Decimals;
- Data Interpretation;
- Equations;
- Quantitative Data;
- Increases / Decreases;
- Speed / Distance / Time;
- Mean / Mode / Median / Range;
- Box and Whisker Plots;
- Statistics;
- Currency;
- Mass / Density / Volume;
- Stem and Leaf Diagrams.

Whilst we have provided you with an array of questions, your Numerical Reasoning test will be tailored to the job for which you are applying, and so the questions may not be the same, but will test the same skills and knowledge in terms of an advanced level of mathematics.

Question 1

Mineral water is classified on the basis of the amount of dissolved solid materials it contains. The chart shows the codes of different levels of total dissolved solids (TDS) and the number of mineral water bottles for each code sold at a store.

MINERAL WATER BOTTLES		
Code	TDS (mg/l)	Number of bottles
TDS 1	Less than 50	52
TDS 2	Greater than or equal to 50 but less than 500	85
TDS 3	Greater than or equal to 500 but less than 1,500	65
TDS 4	Greater than or equal to 1,500	50

What fraction of the total number of bottles sold at the store with TDS greater than or equal to 50 mg/l, have the code TDS 4?

A. $1/5$

B. $1/6$

C. $2/4$

D. $1/4$

E. $3/5$

Question 2

Government spending on "Defence Services" and "Transport Services" was 31 billion pounds and 6.4 billion pounds respectively for the year 2010-2011. In the same year, spending on "Education Services" was 150% of the spending on "Defence Services". The spending on "Defence Services", "Transport Services" and "Education Services" constituted 15% of the total spending by the Government.

What was the approximate total spending of the Government for the year 2010-2011?

A. 540 billion pounds

B. 559 billion pounds

C. 432 billion pounds

D. 380 billion pounds

E. 700 billion pounds

Question 3

Here is some information about the costs of purchasing land. Prime farmland is £7,500 per acre. Building land is £1.1 million per hectare.

1 hectare = 10,000 m² = 2.47 acres

A plot of building land is square. The length of one side of the plot is 80m.

Which one of the amounts below is closest in value to the cost of buying the plot?

A. £704,000

B. £568,000

C. £850,000

D. £902,000

E. £400,000

Question 4

The length of one side of a square is $\sqrt{8} + \sqrt{12}$ cm. Work out the area of the square.

Question 5

Find $f(9)$ for the function $f(x) = (x + 14)^2$

Question 6

Samuel's walk is represented by a straight line graph.

At time $t = 4$ hours, he has walked a distance of $d = 20$ kilometres.

At time $t = 5.5$ hours, he has walked a distance of $d = 27.5$ kilometres.

Work out the equation of the line in the form $d = mt + c$.

Question 7

The table shows information about the heights of a group of people.

Height (h, cm)	Frequency
140 < h ≤ 160	100
160 < h ≤ 180	84
180 < h ≤ 200	60
200 < h ≤ 220	12

Draw a histogram to represent the information above.

Question 8

Using your answer to question 7, estimate the number of people between 145 cm and 190 cm tall.

Question 9

Find the centre and the radius of the following circle:

$$(x - 2)^2 + (y - 4)^2 = 25$$

Question 10

Solve the simultaneous equations:

$$-6x + 8y = -35$$

$$2x + 3y = -11$$

Question 11

Work out the missing side length labelled *l* for the triangle below.

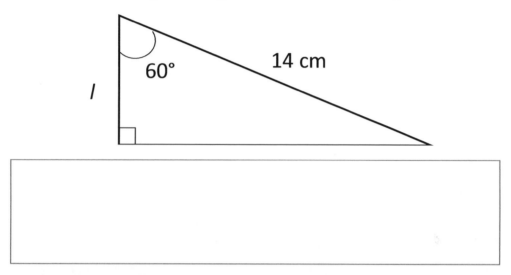

Question 12

Solve the following quadratic equation:

$$6x^2 - 9x + 1 = 0$$

Give your answer to 3 s.f.

Question 13

Kent Police have put out a tender for energy services. Below are quotes from 3 suppliers.

Energy services	Supplier 1 Total cost over 2 years (£)	Supplier 2 Total cost over 6 years (£)	Supplier 3 Total cost over 1 year (£)
Home central heating	6,800	22,500	4,500
Business central heating	8,000	42,000	7,750
Boiler repairs and maintenance	4,500	18,000	2,350

What percentage of the total quote provided by Supplier 3 accounts for business central heating services? Give your answer to 1 decimal place.

A	B	C	D	E
50.1%	53.1%	54.1%	57.1%	48.1%

Question 14

You leave your house at 10:05. You travel for half an hour at 50 mph. When you reach the motorway, the traffic forces you to drive at 15 mph for 12 minutes. After the traffic clears, you continue your journey at 50 mph and arrive at your destination at 11:25.

a) How far do you travel in total? Your answer should be to the nearest mile.

b) How long does the third part of your journey, after the traffic has cleared, take?

Question 15

Below is a table listing the percentage changes in earnings from 2014 to 2016 for five different companies.

COMPANY	Percentage Change from 2014 to 2015	Percentage Change from 2015 to 2016
Company A	+22%	+12%
Company B	+34%	-5%
Company C	-24%	+20%
Company D	-10%	-10%
Company E	+13%	+43%

Using the above table, if company D earned £620,000 in 2014, how much money did the company make in 2016?

Question 16

Using the graph below, plot the following inequalities. Shade in the region which satisfies all three inequalities.

- $y \geq x$
- $y \leq 4$
- $y \geq 8 - 4x$

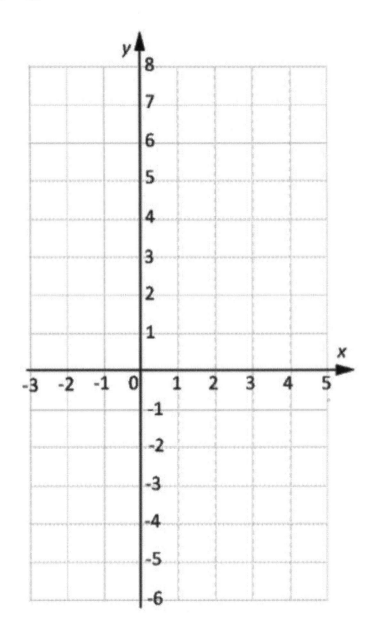

Question 17

The following table shows the daily earnings of an independent book publishing company.

Earnings (x)	Frequency
$500 \leq x < 540$	
$540 \leq x < 560$	
$560 \leq x < 570$	100
$570 \leq x < 600$	180
$600 \leq x < 640$	80
$640 \leq x < 700$	360

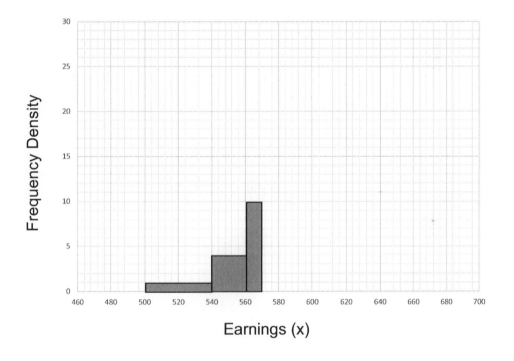

Complete the above frequency table and draw the missing bars on the histogram.

Question 18

Sarah draws two shapes – a square and a circle. The area of the square is 49 cm².

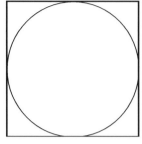

She then makes a pattern using the two shapes which looks like this:

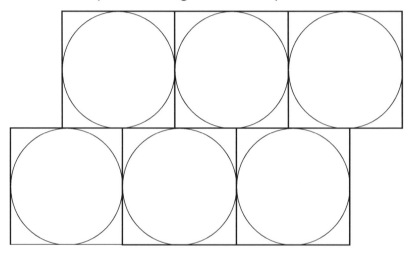

Work out the total surface area which is covered by circles. Round your final answer to 2 decimal places.

Question 19
Work out the inverse function to $f(x)$:

$$f(x) = 8 - 14x$$

Question 20
Below is a circle. Work out the area of the circle. Use the approximation Pi = 3.1 in your calculation.

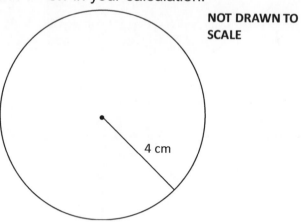

NOT DRAWN TO SCALE

4 cm

ANSWERS TO NUMERICAL REASONING (ADVANCED SECTION 1)

Q1. Q1. D = ¼

EXPLANATION = first, you need to work out the denominator of the fraction. You are trying to work out the total number of bottles sold at the store with TDS greater than or equal to 50, so you need to add up the following:

- 85 + 65 + 50 = 200 (you add up these numbers because these numbers have TDS 50 or above).

You then to work out the numerator of the fraction. You are working out how many bottles have the code TDS 4. According to the table, there are 50 bottles with the code TDS 4.

So the fraction would look like: $^{50}/_{200}$. Simplified, this would be $^1/_4$

Q2. B = 559 billion pounds

EXPLANATION = first, you need to work out what the total was for "Education Services". You know that this was 50% more than the spending for "Defence Services".

- 31 billion x 1.5 = 46.5 billion pounds

You then need to add up all of the costs:

- 31 + 6.4 + 46.5 = 83.9 billion pounds

Step 3 = you know that the above amount (83.9 billion pounds) constituted 15% of the total spending. So now you need to work out the overall total.

- 83.9 x 100 ÷ 15 = 559.33333 billion pounds.

So the approximate value would be 559 billion pounds.

Q3. A = £704,000

EXPLANATION = first you need to multiply 80 by 80 to give you the area:

- 80 x 80 = 6,400m²

Converting 6,400m² to hectares = 6,400 ÷ 10,000 = 0.64 hectares

Multiply this by the price of building land:

- 0.64 x 1,100,000 = £704,000

Q4. 20 + 8√6

EXPLANATION = to work out the area:

$(\sqrt{8} + \sqrt{12})^2 = (\sqrt{8} + \sqrt{12})(\sqrt{8} + \sqrt{12})$

$= (\sqrt{8})^2 + 2\sqrt{8}\sqrt{12} + (\sqrt{12})^2$

$= 8 + 2\sqrt{96} + 12$

$= 20 + 2\sqrt{16}\sqrt{6}$

$= 20 + 8\sqrt{6}$

Q5. 529

EXPLANATION = Put $x = 9$ into the function:

$f(9) = (9 + 14)^2 = 23^2 = 529$

Q6. *d* = 5*t*

EXPLANATION = $\dfrac{d2-d1}{t2-t1} = \dfrac{27.5-20}{5.5-4} = \dfrac{7.5}{1.5} = 5$

So the equation so far = *d* = 5*t* + *c*.

Now substitute (4, 20) into the equation and solve for *c*.

d = 5*t* + *c* ⇒ 20 = 5 x 4 + *c* ⇒ *c* = 30 – 20 = 0

d = 5*t*

Q7.

Height (h, cm)	Frequency	Frequency Density
140 < *h* ≤ 160	100	100 ÷ 20 = 5
160 < *h* ≤ 180	84	84 ÷ 20 = 4.2
180 < *h* ≤ 200	60	60 ÷ 20 = 3
200 < *h* ≤ 220	12	12 ÷ 20 = 0.6

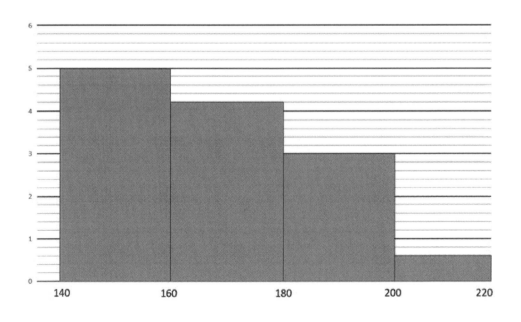

Q8. 189 people

EXPLANATION = between 145 cm and 160 cm

- $5 \times (160 - 145) = 5 \times 15 = 75$

All of the $160 < h \leq 180$ class is included = 84

Between 180 cm and 190 cm =

- $3 \times (190 - 180) = 3 \times 10 = 30$

So the estimate is = 75 + 84 + 30 = 189 people

Q9. Centre of the circle (2, 4) and the radius = 5

EXPLANATION = A circle with centre (a, b) and radius r has an equation of $(x - a)^2 + (y - b)^2 = r^2$. In our equation a = 2, b = 4 and $r^2 = 25$

That means the centre of the circle is (2, 4) and the radius is 5.

Q10. $x = 0.5$ and $y = -4$

EXPLANATION =

- (Equation 1) = $-6x + 8y = -35$ (Equation 2) = $2x + 3y = -11$

- $-6x + 8y = -35$ $6x + 9y = -33$

- $-6z + 6x + 8y + 9y = (-35) + (-33)$

- $17y = -68$ $y = -4$

Substitute $y = -4$ into equation 1 = $-6(x) + 8(-4) = -35$

- $-6x - 32 = -35$ $-6x = -35 + 32$ $-6x = -3$

- $x = 0.5$

Q11. 7

EXPLANATION = $\cos 60° = \dfrac{l}{14}$ $\Rightarrow l = 14 \times \cos 60° = 7$

Q12. x = 1.38 or x = 0.12

EXPLANATION = $6x^2 - 9x + 1 = 0 \Rightarrow a = 6, b = -9, c = 1$

$$x_{1,2} = \frac{-(-9) \pm \sqrt{(-9)^2 - 4 \times 6 \times 1}}{2 \times 6}$$

$$x_{1,2} = \frac{9 \pm \sqrt{81 - 24}}{12} = \frac{9 \pm \sqrt{57}}{12}$$

So $x_1 = \dfrac{9 + \sqrt{57}}{12}$ = 1.38 to 3 s.f.

Or $x_2 = \dfrac{9 - \sqrt{57}}{12}$ = 0.12 to 3 s.f.

Q13. B = 53.1%

EXPLANATION = 4,500 + 7,750 + 2,350 = 14,600.

7,750 ÷ 14,600 x 100 = 53.08.

Rounded to 53.1%

Q14.

a) 59.7 miles

EXPLANATION = Part 1 = 50 mph x 0.5 hrs = 25 miles

Part 2 = 15 mph x (12 ÷ 60) = 3 miles

Part 3 = 50 mph x (38 ÷ 60) = 31.7 miles.

25 + 3 + 31.7 = 59.7 miles

b) 38 minutes

Q15. £502,200

EXPLANATION = 620,000 ÷ 100 x 90 = 558,000

558,000 ÷ 100 x 105 = 502,200

Q16.

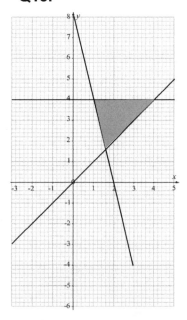

Q17.

The two missing gaps in the table are 40 and 80.

The bar for 560-570 has a frequency density of 10.

The bar for 570-600 has a frequency density of 6.

The bar for 600-640 has a frequency density of 2.

The bar for 640-700 has a frequency density of 6.

Frequency density = frequency ÷ class width

Q18. 230.88

Area of a circle = Pi x radius²

Radius of the circle = 7 ÷ 2 = 3.5

$3.5^2 = 12.25$

Pi x 12.25 = 38.4845

38.4845 x 6 = 230.907 = 230.91 to 2 decimal places.

Q19. $\dfrac{8-x}{14}$

EXPLANATION = f(x) = 8 – 14x

x = 8 – 14y $\Rightarrow$ y = $\dfrac{8-x}{14}$

So f^1(x) = $\dfrac{8-x}{14}$

Q20. 49.6

EXPLANATION = 3.1 x 4 x 4 = 49.6

NUMERICAL

ADVANCED

(SECTION 2)

Question 1

C is a curve. This curve has the equation $4y^3 + 20y + 4 = x$

Find $\dfrac{dy}{dx}$ in terms of y.

Question 2

Given that $\sin\theta = \dfrac{\sqrt{6}}{4}$, find the exact value of $\sin 6\theta$.

Question 3

Work out how many integers, n, where $0 \leq n < 1{,}000$ are NOT divisible by 2 or 5.

Question 4

A dance battle is arranged for 2^n dancers. The tournament sees only the winners in any given round proceed to the next stage. Opponents in each round except the fnal are drawn at random, and in any match either player has a probability 0.5 of winning. Two dancers are chosen at random before the frst round.

Work out the probability in terms of n that they will compete against each other in the first round.

Question 5

Solve the simultaneous equations:

$$3x - 2y = 9$$

$$x + 4y = 10$$

Question 6

Show that, in the diagram below, cos α = $\dfrac{63}{65}$

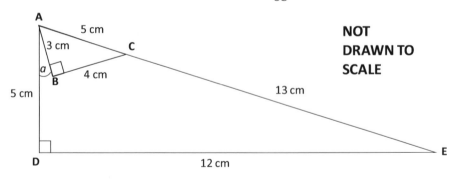

NOT DRAWN TO SCALE

Question 7

In triangle ABC, $\overrightarrow{AB}$ = 4i - 3j and $\overrightarrow{AC}$ = i - 3j

Work out the value of <BAC in degrees to 1 d.p.

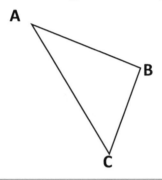

Question 8

Write $6x^2 - 4x = -4$ in the form $p(x + q)^2 + r = 0$

Question 9

Find the length AC in the triangle below. Write your answer to 1 decimal place.

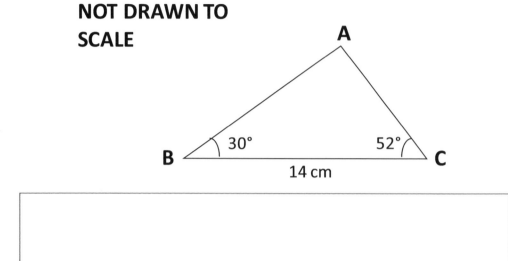

NOT DRAWN TO SCALE

A

30°   52°

B

C

14 cm

Question 10

Solve the simultaneous equations:

$$y = 14 - x$$

$$x - y = 8$$

Question 11

A straight line $y = 4x - 8$ meets the x-axis at point A. Work out the equation of the line with gradient $\frac{1}{3}$ that passes through point A.

Write your answer in the form $ax + by + c = 0$, where a, b and c are integers.

Question 12

A cuboid box is made from 63m² of cardboard. The box has a horizontal base and no top. The height of the box is x metres. The two opposite vertical faces are squares.

Show that the volume of the box is given by $V = 21x - 2/3x^3$

Question 13

Find the coordinates of the stationary points on the curve with the following equation:

$$y = \frac{2}{3}x^3 - 12x^2 + 20x + 2$$

Question 14

If $4x - y = 16$, what is the value of $16^x / 2^y$?

Question 15

Below is an image of an enclosure. If the length of the diagonal BD is 80 metres, work out the angle between the fences AB and BC.

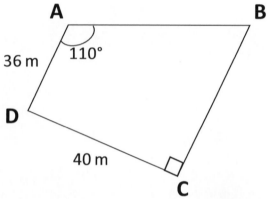

NOT DRAWN TO SCALE

Question 16

Here is some information about the costs of purchasing land.

Prime farmland is £6,500 per acre. Building land is £1.2 million per hectare. The table shows the costs, in thousands of pounds per hectare, of cleaning sites. These are paid in addition to cost of purchasing the land.

End Use / Previous Use	Factories	Sewage works	Scrapyards	Steel works Chemical works
Open space	80	200	400	395
Residential	150	350	500	475
Employment	80	200	175	450
Mixed use	90	258	465	395

1 hectare = 10,000 m² = 2.47 acres.

Building developers buy an old sewage works with an area of 4 acres. They intend to clean the site for residential use. They know they can use an area 1/10th of an acre for a house.

Work out the total cost, to the nearest £, of buying and cleaning the land per house.

Question 17

Find positive integers *a* and *b* such that $3a + 7b = 29$.

Question 18

Evaluate the sum

$$\sum_{10}^{20} (6b - 4)$$

Question 19

Here is some information about the costs of purchasing land. Prime farmland is £7,500 per acre. Building land is £1.1 million per hectare. The table shows the costs, in thousands of pounds per hectare, of cleaning sites. These are paid in addition to the cost of purchasing the land.

End Use / Previous Use	Factories	Sewage works	Scrapyards	Steel works Chemical works
Open space	80	200	400	395
Residential	150	350	500	475
Employment	80	200	175	450
Mixed use	90	258	465	395

1 hectare = 10,000 m² = 2.47 acres

How many whole hectares of prime farmland could be bought for the total cost of buying a one hectare derelict sewage works and cleaning it for residential use?

Question 20

The mean of a set of 10 numbers is 50. The mean of another set of 12 numbers is 42.

Work out the combined mean of both sets of numbers. Write your answer to 2 d.p.

ANSWERS TO NUMERICAL REASONING (ADVANCED SECTION 2)

Q1. $\dfrac{dy}{dx} = \dfrac{1}{12y^2+20}$

EXPLANATION =

$x = 4y^3 + 20y + 4$

$dx/dy = 12y^2 + 20$

$dx/dy = (4 \times 3)y^{3-1} + 20y^{1-1} + 0$

$\dfrac{dy}{dx} = \dfrac{1}{12y^2+20}$

Q2. $-\dfrac{3}{16}\sqrt{15}$

EXPLANATION = $\sin 6\theta = \sin 2\,(3\theta)$

Using the double angle formula $\sin 2x = 2 \sin x \cos x$ to expand $\sin 2(3\theta)$

$\sin 6\theta = 2 \sin 3\theta \cos 3\theta$

Using the triple angle formula $\sin 3x = 3 \sin x - 4 \sin^3 x$ and $\cos 3x = 4 \cos^3 x - 3 \cos x$ to expand $\sin 3\theta$ and $\cos 3\theta$

$\sin 6\theta = 2(3 \sin \theta - 4 \sin^3 \theta)(4 \cos^3 \theta - 3 \cos \theta)$

Given that $\sin \theta = \dfrac{\sqrt{6}}{4}$, then $\cos \theta = \dfrac{\sqrt{10}}{4}$

$\sin 6\theta = 2\left(3\left(\dfrac{\sqrt{6}}{4}\right) - 4\left(\dfrac{\sqrt{6}}{4}\right)^3\right)\left(4\left(\dfrac{\sqrt{10}}{4}\right)^3 - 3\left(\dfrac{\sqrt{10}}{4}\right)\right) = -\dfrac{3}{16}\sqrt{15}$

Q3. 400

EXPLANATION = Integers ending in 1, 3, 7 or 9 will not be divisible by 2 or 5. This is equivalent to 4/10.

The total number of integers is 4/10 of 1,000 = 400.

Q4. $\dfrac{1}{2^{2n} - 2^n}$

EXPLANATION =

The probability of picking the first dancer, D1, is $\dfrac{1}{2^n}$.

The probability of picking the second dancer, D2, is $\dfrac{1}{2^n - 1}$.

The probability of these two dancers competing against each other is:

$$\dfrac{1}{2^n} \times \dfrac{1}{2^n - 1} = \dfrac{1}{2^{2n} - 2^n}.$$

Q5. $x = 4$ and $y = 1.5$

EXPLANATION = Begin by multiplying the equation $x + 4y = 10$ by 3 so that we have the same coefficient of x with the first equation

Equation 1: $3x - 2y = 9$

Equation 2: $3x + 12y = 30$ (after multiplying each term by 3)

Subtract Equation 1 from Equation 2, we have:

$12y - (-2y) = 30 - 9$

$14y = 21$

$y = {}^{21}/_{14} = 1.5$

Substitute the value $y=1.5$ back into the first equation

$3x - (2 \times 1.5) = 9$

$3x - 3 = 9$

$3x = 12$

$x = 4$

Q6. Your working out should be as follows:

Using the two right-angled triangles we can determine the following trigonometric ratios:

$$\sin \angle DAE = \frac{12}{13}, \qquad \cos \angle DAE = \frac{5}{13}$$
$$\sin \angle BAC = \frac{4}{5}, \qquad \cos \angle BAC = \frac{3}{5}$$

Now since $\alpha = \angle DAE - \angle BAC$, we can use the angle subtraction formula for cosine to find $\cos \alpha$:

$$\cos \alpha = \cos(\angle DAE - \angle BAC)$$
$$= \cos \angle DAE \cos \angle BAC + \sin \angle DAE \sin \angle BAC$$
$$= \frac{5}{13} \cdot \frac{3}{5} + \frac{12}{13} \cdot \frac{4}{5}$$
$$= \frac{15}{65} + \frac{48}{65}$$
$$= \frac{63}{65}.$$

Q7. 34.7°

EXPLANATION: First find the dot product $\overrightarrow{AB} \cdot \overrightarrow{AC}$:

$\overrightarrow{AB} \cdot \overrightarrow{AC} = (4 \times 1) + (-3x \ -3) = 4 + 9 = 13$

$|\overrightarrow{AB}| = \sqrt{4^2 + (-3)^2} = \sqrt{25} = 5$ and $|\overrightarrow{AC}| = \sqrt{1^2 + (-3)^2} = \sqrt{10}$. Use the identity $\overrightarrow{AB} \cdot$

$\overrightarrow{AC} = |\overrightarrow{AB}||\overrightarrow{AC}| \cos \emptyset$, where $\emptyset$ is the angle between the vectors:

$5\sqrt{10} \cos \emptyset = 13$

$\emptyset = \cos^{-1} \frac{13}{5\sqrt{10}} \approx 34.7°$

Q8. $6 \left(x - \frac{1}{3}\right)^2 + \frac{10}{3} = 0$

EXPLANATION $= 6x^2 - 4x + 4 = 0$

$6 \left(x^2 - \frac{2}{3}x\right) + 4 = 0$

Since $(x - \frac{1}{3})^2 = x^2 - \frac{2}{3}x + \frac{1}{9}$, we can rewrite $x^2 - \frac{2}{3}x$ as $(x - \frac{1}{3})^2 - \frac{1}{9}$:

$6\left((x - \frac{1}{3})^2 - \frac{1}{9}\right) + 4 = 0$

$6(x - \frac{1}{3})^2 - \frac{1}{9} + 4 = 0$

$6(x - \frac{1}{3})^2 + \frac{10}{3} = 0$

Q9. 7.1 cm

EXPLANATION = Angle BAC = 180 - (30 + 52) = 98°

$\dfrac{AC}{\sin 30} = \dfrac{14}{\sin 98}$

$AC = \dfrac{14}{\sin 98} \times \sin 30$

AC = 7.1 (rounded to 1 d.p.)

Q10. $x = 11$ and $y = 3$

EXPLANATION =

$x - (14 - x) = 8$

$x - 14 + x = 8$

$2x - 14 = 8$

$2x = 8 + 14$

$2x = 22$

$x = 11$

If you substitute that into the equations, you will be able to work out that $y = 3$

Q11. -x + 3y + 2 = 0 or x - 3y - 2 = 0

EXPLANATION = 0 = 4x – 8 So x = 2. A is the point (2, 0).

$3y = x - 2$

$-x + 3y + 2 = 0$

Q12. Your working out should look like this:

EXPLANATION = area = $2x^2 + 3xy$

$63 = 2x^2 + 3xy$

$$y = \frac{63 - 2x^2}{3x}$$

$$V = x^2 \left(\frac{63 - 2x^2}{3x}\right)$$

$$= \frac{x}{3}(63 - 2x^2)$$

$$\text{So } V = 21x - \frac{2}{3}x^3$$

Q13. Your working out should look like this:

EXPLANATION = $(6 + \sqrt{26}, -342.8)$ and $(6 - \sqrt{26}, 10.8)$

$y = \frac{2}{3}x^3 - 12x^2 + 20x + 2$

$\frac{dy}{dx} = (\frac{2}{3} \times 3) x^{3-1} - (12 \times 2)x^{2-1} + (20 \times 1)x^{1-1} + 0$

$\frac{dy}{dx} = 2x^2 - 24x^1 + 20$

$$\frac{dy}{dx} = 0 \Rightarrow 2x^2 - 24x + 20 = 0$$

$$\Rightarrow x^2 - 12x + 10 = 0$$

$$\Rightarrow x = \frac{12 \pm \sqrt{(-12)^2 - 4 \cdot 10}}{2}$$

$$\Rightarrow x = 6 \pm \sqrt{26}.$$

$$y_1 = \frac{2}{3}(6 + \sqrt{26})^3 - 12(6 + \sqrt{26})^2 + 20(6 + \sqrt{26}) + 2 = -342.8$$

$$y_2 = \frac{2}{3}(6 - \sqrt{26})^3 - 12(6 - \sqrt{26})^2 + 20(6 - \sqrt{26}) + 2 = 10.8$$

Q14. 2^{16}

EXPLANATION =

$$\frac{16^x}{2^y} = \frac{(2^4)^x}{2^y} = \frac{2^4 x}{2^y} = 2^{(4x-y)} = \frac{16^x}{2^y} = 2^{16}$$

Q15. $55.0°$

EXPLANATION =

$$\sin \angle DBC = \frac{40}{80}$$
$$\angle DBC = \sin^{-1} 0.5$$
$$= 30°.$$

Now use the sine rule to find $\angle ABD$:

$$\frac{\sin \angle ABD}{36} = \frac{\sin 110°}{80}$$
$$\sin \angle ABD = \frac{36 \sin 110°}{80}$$
$$\angle ABD = \sin^{-1}\left(\frac{36 \sin 110°}{80}\right)$$
$$= 25.01.$$

Then $\angle ABC = \angle DBC + \angle ABD = 30° + 25.01° = 55.0°$ to 1dp.

Q16. £62,753

EXPLANATION = Number of houses = 4 acres $\div \frac{1}{10}$ = 40 houses.

4 acres = $\frac{4}{2.47}$ hectare.

Cost of buying = 1,200,000 x $\frac{4}{2.47}$ = £1,943,319.84

Cost of cleaning = 350,000 x $\frac{4}{2.47}$ = 566,801.62

Total cost = 1,943,319.84 + 566,801.62 = £2,510,121.46

Total cost per house = 2510121.46 ÷ 40 = £62,753.04

To the nearest pound = £62,753

Q17. a = 5, b = 2

EXPLANATION = To solve this, start by considering the possible values of b. We know that b is positive, and b < 5, since 5·7 = 35, which is greater than 29.

If b = 1, then 7b = 7, so 3a + 7 = 29 meaning 3a = 22. This cannot have an integer solution for a, as 22 is not a multiple of 3.

If b = 2, then 7b = 7·2 = 14, so 3a + 14 = 29 meaning 3a = 15. This has solution a = 5. So a possible pair of positive integers a, and b, such that 3a + 7b = 29 is a = 5, b = 2.

There are no other positive integer solutions for a and b to this equation, since if b = 3, 3a = 8, and if b = 4, 3a = 1. Neither of these possibilities has an integer solution for a.

Q18. 946

EXPLANATION =

$\sum_{b=10}^{20}(6b - 4) = (6 \sum_{r=1}^{20} r - \sum_{r=1}^{20} 4) - (6 \sum_{r=1}^{9} r - \sum_{r=1}^{9} 4)$

$(\frac{6}{2} \times 20(21) - 4 \times 20) - (\frac{6}{2} \times 9(10) - 4 \times 9)$

$= (1290 - 80) - (270 - 36) = 1180 - 234 = 946$

Q19. 78

EXPLANATION =

Total cost of buying and cleaning =

- 1,100,000 + 350,000 = 1,450,000 for one hectare.

If total cost is £1,450,000 for one hectare, then the total cost is also £1,450,000 for 2.47 acres (since 1 hectare = 2.47 acres). Total cost for one acre =

- 1,450,000 ÷ 2.47 = £587,044.53

Number of farmland could be bought in acres =

- £587,044.53 ÷ £7,500 = 78.27

The number of whole hectares would be 78.

Q20. 45.64

EXPLANATION =

$$\frac{10 \times 50 + 12 \times 42}{10 + 12} = \frac{1004}{22} = 45.636$$

To 2 d.p. = 45.64

Take a look at our other Reasoning guides!

Each guide is packed full of examples and practice questions, to ensure that you make the most out of your revision time and can aim to achieve 100%!

FOR MORE INFORMATION ON OUR TESTING GUIDES, PLEASE CHECK OUT THE FOLLOWING:

WWW.HOW2BECOME.COM

Get Access To
FREE
Reasoning
Test Questions

www.MyPsychometricTests.co.uk

Printed in Great
Britain
by Amazon

32177325R00108